THE DAD'S SURVIVAL GUIDE

IAN BANKS

Cartoons by James Campbell

THE
BLACKSTAFF
PRESS

BELFAST

ACKNOWLEDGEMENTS

Writing a book called *The Dad's Survival Guide* was surprisingly difficult even for an Old Dad. There were many false starts and disappointments, not unlike becoming a dad itself. It took the help of many to bring the book to a successful conclusion. Dr Paul Smith started the ball rolling while Sally Taylorson of the Health Development Agency kept the moss off it. The Family Planning Association gave it a shove in the right, safer, direction and the Doctor Patient Partnership looked at it from both sides. Peter Baker gave it a men's health spin and provided much needed encouragement to keep it in the air. Jack O'Sullivan has heard it all before, yet still stayed awake while checking the script. Northern Ireland's premier Jubilee and Lagan Valley maternity units helped provide the wonderful quotes from dads and gave the ball a good strong push this time. My particular thanks to all the fathers who took the time to reply to my questionnaires. Blackstaff Press – especially Patsy Horton – and James Campbell caught the ball on the bounce and turned it into a book. Amazing.

Much of the insight came from own children, Jenny, John, Beth and Peter – practice has the edge over theory any time. It takes two to tango and literally none of this would have happened without Hilary. 'Why don't we have kids?' she said seventeen years ago, putting the ball firmly in my court. And the rest, as they say, is nappies.

First published in 2001 by
The Blackstaff Press Limited
Wildflower Way, Apollo Road, Belfast BT12 6TA, Northern Ireland

© Text, Ian Banks, 2001
© Cartoons, James Campbell, 2001

Printed in Ireland by Betaprint

A CIP catalogue record for this book
is available from the British Library

ISBN 0-85640-696-1

www.blackstaffpress.com

In a previous life Ian Banks was a television repair man. He might not be able to cure you but he can do wonders for your vertical hold. He has four children, one of which he delivered himself. 'Not quite the same as childbirth but at least I got to shout "push".' While working part-time as a family doctor and casualty officer in Belfast, he also represents GPs for the British Medical Association and is a member of the Council for the UK. Ian is the offical spokesman on men's health issues for the BMA, president of the Men's Health Forum and has been the medical editor for *The Men's Health Magazine* for the last six years. In 1996 he wrote the BBC book, *The Trouble with Men*, to accomany the television series of the same name. It was followed by *Ask Dr Ian About Men's Health* (Blackstaff Press), *The Good Patient Guide* (BBC), *The Children's Health Guide* (BBC), *Get Fit with Brittas* (BBC), *Men's Health in General Practice* (Haymarket), *Ask Dr Ian About Sex* (Blackstaff Press) and the NHS 50th anniversary book from the NHSE/HEA, *The Home Medicine Guide*. He is also the author of *The NHS Direct Healthcare Guide* (Radcliffe Medical Press) and designed their website. Ian is the editor of *The Men's Health Journal* and *The European General Practice Clinical Journal*. Home is a small GM-free farm in Northern Ireland.

For
mum and dad
and their four grandchildren,
Jenny, John, Beth and Peter

Contents

Introduction

So I went into the interview vaguely aware of a faint fishy smell which I put down to poor cleaning at the hospital at which I was applying for a job. I thought it best not to comment on it just in case it happened to be a little known aftershave for senior consultants. Only when I got home did my wife notice Jenny's vomit down the back of my jacket. I still landed the job but I was more careful in future about tight hugs for luck.

As with men's health, ignorance is the biggest single enemy in giving men a greater role as fathers. Us men have traditionally been expected to be less than knowledgeable about raising children. Most of it is self-perpetuating. Men work, earn money, make children. Women look after men, keep the home, have children, or at least they used to until equality came along. Men were typecast as breadwinners, disciplinarians, aloof and often absent figures. Now many men are working in part-time employment and more women than ever are leaving the home to work in jobs formerly thought the sole preserve of men.

Times certainly are changing and most of us are starting to want more and wonder where the hell the years went between potty training and going to pot. This will require changes in the way employers and government provide for dads to give and get the most out of having kids. It's not just dads that benefit. Our partners and kids stop getting such a bum deal. So we lose our traditional domination over jobs, but think of the plus side like, erm, daytime TV. Hmm.

It's like this: we haven't got a choice so we better get used to the idea and turn it into what we want. Even the European Union has committed itself to men as dads.

Member States should promote and encourage, with due respect for freedom of the individual, increased participation by men [in the care and upbringing of children], in order to achieve a more equal sharing of parental responsibilities between men and women.

Not exactly rhyming slang but it's hard to miss the drift. Basically it's a 'get your ass into gear notice' for governments. Easy to say, if not to read, but a bit more difficult to put into practice. We are talking serious vested interest here on all sides. Even some women see men's increased interest in parenting as a threat rather than a chance for freedom.

Not all of us have the luxury of a stable family with in-laws previously considered only marginally more useful than a nasty contagious disease suddenly transformed into baby minders. An increasing number of dads bring up their kids on their own. Character building maybe, but so is being a member of the SAS and they only have people trying to kill them.

If you are the reluctant or undecided dad it's worth knowing that every major charity working in the area of childcare is highlighting the importance of the role of fathers and their involvement with their children. Research by some very clever people indeed shows that having an available loving dad can make big differences at school, with more positive attitudes towards learning and a higher success rate in examinations. Not surprisingly the people who know about these things reckon that men who are the sons of actively involved fathers have a more secure self-image than those whose fathers had little involvement in parenting.

Look guys, this is not war. Forget the battle of the sexes. We are not asking women to contemplate the Alamo or Rourke's Drift. We've got a sneaky hunch that there could be more fun being carers, rather than just providers.

> I felt like a 'hole in the wall' cash dispenser. The kids were in bed when I went out to work and in bed when I came home. At the weekends they went to stay with their grandma.
>
> Divorced father of three

Superglue bonding

OK, we can't really offer our newborn offspring nearly as much as their mum but this bonding thing can work one way for a while, or at least until milk becomes boring.

Over the past couple of decades, men have been increasingly 'allowed' to be present during the birth of their child although some midwives feel it is not always helpful. I do a roaring trade in stitching men's scalps who pass out either from hunger or the sight of blood during the birth of their children. For some men it is a wonderful experience; for others it is on par with being at the wrong end of the Texas chainsaw massacre.

Don't panic

Fathers do not posses a middle ground when it comes to their children's illnesses. We either dismiss the problem as trivial or carry them, personally, into the nearest accident and emergency department and demand an intensive care bed immediately. Hypocrisy oozes from every pore in my body as I write this. My wife Hilary brought our eldest son into casualty, where I was on duty, after he fell from his bunk bed. A quick, some might say cursory, examination showed no fractures of his wrist and I told her so. 'I want an X-ray,' she demanded with a look that has turned the world's bureaucrats into pillars of salt. 'Look love,' I retorted, summoning all the professional glop I could muster, 'I'm the doctor here and I say it isn't broken.' 'I still want an X-ray.' Feeling a distinct salty taste coming on, I led the way, with bad grace, to the X-ray department where they, of course, confirmed fractures of both bones at the wrist.

Having information is the key to enabling fathers to make judgments on the degree of illness. Most books on children's health are directed towards mothers or female carers who generally do not possess this male 'all or nothing' brain pattern. Paradoxically, most men have car manuals and will read them avidly despite never actually intending to 'take the head off and de-coke the valves'. So when something does go wrong with the car, as it inevitably does, there is a greater level of insight than there might have been otherwise.

This is your workshop manual on surviving fatherhood. It covers everything you need to know about the early years. You will not need a screwdriver, hammer or one of those thingys for taking stones out of a horse's hoof. Thankfully children do not come as flat-packs or there would be an awful lot of kids with extra ears and back-to-front knees. This book will take you through the process of deciding whether to have children and the problems that can occur.

Psychologists tell us that moving house rates very high on the Richter scale for stress, but the move from the womb places a huge amount of stress on baby, mum and dad, so knowing what is happening and why, will help you survive this earthquake of emotion

Life was once much simpler for dads when it came to looking after their children. Simpler, but much less fun. Coping at home and in the great outdoors, and getting to know your child is not passed on through genes. Not much of it is passed on from father to son either, so this book takes a good look at all of this – and yes, you can try this at home.

Serious illness is on the decline among children in the developed nations and every sniff or sneeze doesn't herald some life-threatening condition. There is no shortage of relatively harmless complaints that your child will suffer from and the A to Z of children's problems and illnesses will help you through difficult spots and frequent visits to the loo.

Recognising the difference between trivial infections such as a bad cold and the real nasties is vital and the section gives you confidence to either call for help or watch and wait for nature to take its almost benign course.

I hope that you will have read this book before your child's head comes off and coked-up valves fall out all over the kitchen floor, just like the last time you used the kitchen table for running repairs. Good luck, Dad.

Why be a dad?

Darwin got it right first time. The survival of the species has got nothing to do with insight and everything to do with a red mist. Just as well. If you could sample the anticipation of waiting for a teenager to return home safely from a night out or the pleasure of long-distance driving during the family holiday, there might be more seed hitting stony ground. Men are not always forthcoming when asked their reason for having children. Not having the right change for the machine in the men's loo is a common reply. Where there was more planning and less chance involved men say: 'My wife wanted a child' or 'I wanted my name to live on.'

Increasingly, though, men are approaching dad status a little more positively, even if it is 'that's the last one, I'm positive' kind of positivism. Like women, we are having children much later in life – about ten years later over the last two decades.

Most developed nations view contraception as sensible if not essential. Family planning is big business and we are getting good at it, with families averaging 2.5 children keeping the population more or less constant. Older people will outnumber children by four times over the next twenty years. Obviously sex and procreation are separate things to most people, especially, I suspect, men. Just as well – it would be standing room only for humans if late night television is anything to go by.

Pressure to have kids can come from many directions, not least the rest of the family. There is still the 'have 'em soon before it's too late' mentality. Even worse if the woman is older than her partner. Part of the rationale comes from the increasing danger of genetic malformations with both older women and men. Paradoxically more malformed children are born to much younger women simply because there is a less perceived need for screening. While lambasting women for having children after menopause using modern techniques, society sees older male fathers as a positive asset. The number of kids born to women in their late thirties is increasing by eighteen thousand per year. Women are voting with their wombs.

Deep impact

Not many of us really, really realise just how much we change once there is someone else in the picture. Cash becomes more of a worry. The days of spending the pay packet within the first two days are gone forever yet most men rate their loss of 'freedom', increasing responsibility and influence on sex more highly than the drain on the bank account. Financial advisers reckon having children is the most expensive personal

> I never told my wife but I was absolutely horrified when she told me she was pregnant.
>
> New dad

investment we will ever make, more costly even than buying a house. Ask any guy with teenage daughters and a phone.

Risk taking decreases – car driving and the insurance companies are especially quick to pick this up. During World War II unmarried young men flew the relatively cheap fighters and were encouraged to take risks while married older men, preferably with children, flew the expensive bombers with their highly trained crews. Pretty sneaky stuff. Even jobs in industry and the public services often reflect this shift in behaviour and most men will recognise it. Absenteeism from work declines, job migration falls, and sick time drops.

Youth versus experience

Young dads

You are going to need all the youth you can muster, especially when the jet lag from the long-haul trips to the kitchen for night-time feeds starts to kick in. On the other hand you will be able to take part in their games as they get older without snapping your Achilles tendon and be young enough to enjoy regained independence once they leave home. You are also less likely to employ a crowbar to lever the remaining son out of the family home. An obstetrician once reported that snoring during pregnancy can be fatal. As an older dad I can tell you that snoring during conception can be pretty life-threatening as well. For you conception will be easier with less fear of genetic malformation not to mention cramp.

Before you shout 'brace yourself, darling', just a word in your ear. You may be losing the best years of your life.

Along comes responsibility, a whole new look at snowboarding, lost mates, especially the snowboarding variety, financial commitments when your earning power is at its lowest and, of course, that haunting fragrance of damp nappy women can spot at a hundred paces.

> We were both still in sixth form when our son was born. I was intending to go to university but instead took a job at my father's firm. I don't regret what happened I just feel we mortgaged our youth a bit.
>
> Dad with three kids, now an Open University student

Middle-aged dads

Don't look so smug. Yes it's easy to see the advantages of kids while you are in your thirties with more earning power, a good taste of the free unfettered youth, and your parents still around to do all the babysitting while you swan off to breakaway holidays in Iberia, but wait a second, mate. Work pressure is at its highest during your middle age especially increasing competition from women in the job market. The lifelong post is no more. Keeping on track with your career might be difficult with a few kids in the equation. Paradoxically, you might spend more time securing their future than actually being with them.

Older dads

Nothing comes near an old dad for smug. We value age as a source of wisdom and patience and of course it is theoretically possible to become a dad no matter how old you are. You don't even need to worry about the sweaty bit either, even if masturbation is not possible because of erectile dysfunction. Prostatic massage can often produce sufficient ejaculate for assisted insemination. I must tell you, however, that there is only one route for a physician's massaging finger and it isn't your ear. However, most doctors are merciful and will use an

> She-who-must-be-obeyed doesn't seem to realise where all the money comes from for all the clothes and toys. Someone has to go out and earn it the hard way. I can't earn money sitting at home all day.
>
> Dad with a wife, four children and a 32-ton lorry to keep, as he put it

anaesthetic. Finance is also usually less of a problem and your decision to have kids is less likely to be based on an irrational red haze. Smaller family size is also more likely, increasing personal contact and lessening the burden of responsibility.

Just a thought, however, before dispensing with the Zimmer for a few vital moments. Death, the grim reaper, is more likely to rob your children of your presence at an earlier age. You are less likely to take part in their activities and conception may be more difficult with an increased risk of genetic malformation. Even so, average life expectancy is increasing and the older dad of the industrial revolution, with a life expectancy of less than forty years, is the middle-aged father of today.

For many of us there will be no choice and serendipity will be the master.

> When my wife told me she was pregnant I thought great, but then I thought of my sport and how dangerous it was.
>
> Famous racing driver who subsequently left his wife because he felt too irresponsible to be a father. He still races cars.

Timing is everything
Planning ahead with contraception

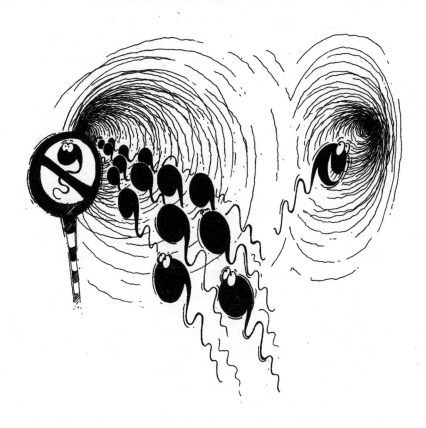

Family planning

Now is not the time to seriously consider the 'wham, bam, cheerio mam' technique. Men have a macho attitude towards most things at the best of times but especially to sex. Why does only one sperm succeed in fertilising the egg? Simple, all the rest refuse to stop and ask for directions.

Contraception

There are numerous methods of contraception, most of which, it has to be said, depend more on the woman than the man. There is, however, no excuse for ignorance and no reason for not being involved in decisions about contraception. Not only is there a difference in methods of contraception, there is a significant difference in the protection each method provides.

The condom

Society is increasingly accepting the condom as one of the normal requirements of modern life. Condoms are now readily available in supermarkets, from garages, through slot machines, as well as in pharmacies. Colours and flavours make interesting options. Some condoms are lubricated with spermicide, which increases their effectiveness as a contraceptive and provides a degree of protection from sexually transmitted infections (STIs). Even in a stable relationship, the protection provided by condoms can be valuable, as thrush (candida) is a common infection of the urinary tract for both men and women, particularly after prolonged courses of antibiotics, and can be sexually transmitted. Hermetically sealed, the modern condom will remain usable for a long time (look for the kite mark of the British Standards Institute). Once the seal is broken they should be used quite soon as the rubber will perish on exposure to the air and the lubricant will dry, making it difficult to put on.

Putting a condom on in the correct manner is important. Air should be excluded from the end of the condom as it can cause it to burst or slip off as the penis shrinks in size after ejaculation. Sharp finger nails are a hazard and only the soft finger pulps should be used to unroll the condom on to the penis.

Perhaps the single biggest stated reason for not using condoms is the widely held belief that they inhibit spontaneous sex. Foreplay is an important part of enjoyable sexual activity and partners can involve the condom in this way. Fears that they reduce the sensitivity of sexual experience have not been supported by experiment. Most of the problem lies in the psychological inhibition some men have over their use.

The female condom

The condom for women is relatively new, but regular users report favourably and many men prefer them to the male condom. It is much larger in diameter than the male condom and has two flexible rings at each end. The smaller ring fits inside the vagina while the outer much larger ring remains on the outside of the vagina. After ejaculation this outer ring should be twisted to prevent escape of the sperm and gently withdrawn.

The oral contraceptive

Mixed hormonal contraceptive pills mimic pregnancy, thus inhibiting the release of hormones which stimulate the final development and release of ova (eggs) from the ovary. This partly explains why some women suffer the milder symptoms of pregnancy during their use.

The progesterone-only pill discourages sperm from getting anywhere near the womb by maintaining the natural plug in the neck of the cervix which will not allow the passage of sperm while the levels of progesterone are high. This pill has many of the advantages of the mixed pill without the 'pregnancy'. It has, however, to be taken regularly at the same time each day.

While the contraceptive pill is convenient and relatively efficient, there are definite health risks associated with their prolonged use – especially if a woman is over the age of thirty to thirty-five, smokes, is overweight, has a history of either heart disease, high blood pressure, liver disease or elevated cholesterol levels.

Intrauterine contraceptive device (IUCD)

These small plastic devices, inserted by GPs or doctors at family planning clinics, cause a mild inflammation within the womb which renders the lining of the womb unsuitable for implantation by the fertilised egg. They can be left in the uterus (womb) for up to five years although the newer versions which release a measured amount of progesterone (see the oral contraceptive pill), need to be replaced yearly. Most doctors recommend they only be used after the first pregnancy as there is a small risk of infection which can lead to infertility. Some doctors feel they should be used only once a woman has completed her family. They are removed very easily by a doctor and have no effect upon sensation during intercourse.

Hormone implants (for women)

Based upon the same principle as the progesterone-only pill, it is possible to insert, under a local anaesthetic, very small containers of progesterone beneath the skin. The hormone leaches out at a predetermined rate providing complete contraception for around five years.

The male pill

Male contraception is still in its infancy. A male oral contraceptive pill has yet to be passed for human use in the UK although there have been successful trials in China and encouraging results in animal experimentation.

Vasectomy

As a form of contraception, vasectomy has maintained its position as a popular, almost 100 per cent means of preventing unwanted pregnancies. It is, along with the condom, one of the very few ways where a man really does have control over conception. For most men, its single biggest attraction is its lack of intrusion on the actual enjoyment of sexual intercourse, while providing as near absolute contraception that can be achieved.

Risks

Your decision to have a vasectomy will depend upon your age, how many children you already have and the impact any further children may have on your family. Doctors are obviously not keen to perform a vasectomy in men who do not have any children. Similarly, while splitting up with your current partner may be the last thing on your mind, you may want to have more children with a new partner at some later date. It is also worth mentioning that many men who have vasectomies suffer from chronic testicular pain after the operation. At least 10 per cent of men are affected, though some studies show an incidence of around 15–35 per cent. The Royal College of Obstetricians and Gynaecologists now advises that men are warned of this risk before having a vasectomy.

The operation

The operation is relatively simple. Basically, the vas deferens, which conducts sperm from the testes to the penis, is cut and tied off, or clipped at both cut ends. This effectively prevents any further sperm from reaching the penis. A small cut is made through the skin of the scrotum, under either a local or general anaesthetic. Once identified, each vas is cut, a small piece removed, and the cut ends tied off. Each of the segments which have been cut away are sent off to the laboratory to ensure that the correct tubes have been treated and that there is no sign of any serious medical conditions which need attention. Using a couple of stitches or staples, the wound is closed. It takes no more than about fifteen minutes and is extremely safe. Testes do not swell from sperm building up within them.

100 per cent?

Nature can determine when a normal body function has been interfered with. There are a number of cases, thankfully very few, where a successful operation has been confirmed with a definite removal of the vas tissue and yet a few years later the men concerned have fathered a child. It appears that the body is capable of overcoming the surgical intervention by creating fresh canals for the sperm to travel to the penis. It has to be said that the risk is extremely small, but it explains why the form you sign consenting to the operation will not guarantee 100 per cent success. Reversal of a vasectomy is not impossible, but there is a poor success rate; it depends on how long ago this surgery was performed and on the method used. The operation is not available on the NHS.

Female sterilisation

The Fallopian tubes can be cut and tied off or blocked so that eggs cannot pass down them to the uterus (womb). It is extremely effective but carries a greater risk for the woman than a vasectomy does for the man because a general anaesthetic is required and the operation is more invasive. A small piece of the tube is sent for examination to ensure that the correct tube has been blocked. It is possible to reverse the operation but with limited success.

Emergency contraception

Emergency contraception, either in the form of the so-called 'morning after' pill – which must be used within seventy-two hours of unprotected intercourse – or with the insertion of a coil, should only ever be used in an emergency, for instance if a condom tears. The 'morning after' pill can now be bought over-the-counter in chemist shops.

Natural methods

Theoretically, it is only possible for your partner to conceive within seven days of ovulation or twenty-four hours afterwards. Using various tests it is possible to estimate the time of ovulation. By using a thermometer and a chart it is possible to detect the sudden rise in temperature of around 0.5 degrees celsius which occurs at ovulation. Readings must be taken first thing in the morning, before any exercise, food, drink or even smoking. Obviously, this can be confused by increases in temperature from a cold or flu. The 'safe' phase – when the risk of pregnancy is at its lowest – begins on the morning of the third day of increased temperature. This can be made more accurate by testing the cervical mucous which becomes thicker and less sticky, tending to resist being drawn out between the fingers, just after ovulation.

> Don't get me wrong. I wasn't annoyed. I just would have liked a bit of warning.
>
> New dad, after being shown the first ultrasound scan confirming twins

16

Compared to the other methods described, the 'natural' method is not very safe and requires a degree of self-control which may not be present in every man, or woman.

Of thirty dads attending a parenting class in a busy maternity unit in Northern Ireland, only one admitted to taking any precautions before his child was conceived. 'Yes, condoms. They didn't work, obviously.'

I have some good news, no really . . .

Don't expect to be quite as ecstatic as your partner when she tells you her little surprise. For most of us it really is a surprise and not one that competes well with a 5–0 away score. You can usually recognise the guy who has just heard the news as he walks around in work with a fixed grin and spontaneous hair loss.

Women just love to say, 'I've a wonderful surprise for you.' At a stroke this defeats the whole point of 'family planning'. The last thing you should be, chum, is surprised. After all it was your idea, wasn't it?

Sub-fertility

For some couples, the problem is not one of preventing children but rather the difficulty they have in producing a child. With improved awareness of contraception, the number of babies for adoption has fallen and there have been greater attempts made to correct or alleviate sub-fertility for men and women by various means.

Out of every ten couples trying for children, eight achieve pregnancy within a year, one couple will conceive within two years and the remaining couple will need medical help. Many doctors will not consider referring a couple for infertility investigations until they have been trying for around two years while under thirty-five years and one year if the couple are over thirty-five years.

Erectile dysfunction and infertility

Confusion still surrounds the distinction between impotence and infertility. Impotence is the inability to perform the sexual act for whatever reason, including an inability to have an erection. There are many causes, ranging from the psychological to the physical. Some men may have erections while asleep yet be unable to do so during the sexual act. For those who suffer from certain neurological conditions, such as diabetes, impotence can be an unhappy result. Being impotent does not necessarily also mean you are infertile. A man who is infertile is unable to produce sperm which are capable of fertilising a woman's egg.

In fact, most doctors now talk of 'sub' or 'reduced' fertility and may even apply this to a couple who are experiencing problems with producing a child rather than to an individual.

Timing conception

For pregnancy to happen, the man's sperm needs to meet an egg produced by the woman. Ovulation (release of an egg) occurs twelve to sixteen days before a woman's period starts. The egg lives for about a day and sperm can live for up to seven days. So there is only a short time in each month when you are most likely to conceive. It may take up to a year to get pregnant, so don't worry if your partner is not pregnant after a couple of months. It's not true that abstaining from sex means you will 'save up' sperm, so have sex as often as you want to.

If you've been having sex two or three times a week without success after six months you might want to find out the time when your partner is most fertile (ovulation).

- Work out with your partner the number of days in her menstrual cycle. The menstrual cycle starts on the first day of a period and ends the day before the next period starts. Count back twelve to sixteen days from when your partner expects her next period to estimate when ovulation occurs.

- Your partner can check the fluid from her vagina (cervical mucus) as this changes during the month and is wetter, thinner and slippery around ovulation.

- Ovulation predictor kits which test a woman's urine are fairly simple to use and can be bought at pharmacies. They are of limited value if your partner has irregular periods or a menstrual cycle that is shorter than twenty-one days or longer than thirty-five days. In this case talk to your doctor.

How long you should spend trying for pregnancy before seeking help depends to some extent on the medical histories and age of you and your partner.

Ring NHS Direct or attend your family planning clinic if your partner:

- has irregular periods or if the menstrual cycle is shorter or longer than twenty-one to thirty-five days
- finds intercourse is painful
- has a previous history of pelvic inflammatory disease
- has ever had abdominal surgery
- has ever had chlamydia or another sexually transmitted infection
- is underweight or overweight
- is aged over thirty-five

Or if you:

- have had an operation on the testes or had treatment for testicular cancer or an undescended testicle
- have ever had chlamydia or another sexually transmitted infection
- have a history of mumps after puberty
- are very overweight

Be prepared to discuss questions such as:

- your general medical health
- your partner's menstrual cycle
- previous methods of contraception
- any previous pregnancies/miscarriages/abortions
- any infections, including sexually transmitted infections
- how often you have intercourse

Causes of infertility and possible treatments

- a woman who has difficulty in ovulating may need a course of drugs

- a woman not producing eggs may need another woman to donate eggs (this is not routinely offered)

- a woman with blocked Fallopian tubes may need surgery or assisted conception

- a man with low numbers and/or poor-quality sperm may need assisted conception to aid fertilisation using his own sperm, or sperm from a donor may be needed

There may be other, less common causes and a couple may have a combination of problems, so investigations need to be completed even if one problem is found at an early stage. Most problems can be helped, with varying degrees of success. Sometimes, even after full investigations, the reason for infertility cannot be found but assisted conception treatment may still be successful.

Visiting your GP gives you and your partner the opportunity to ask about the possible investigations and treatments, waiting lists and any costs. You can then decide if you want to go ahead with tests and/or treatment. You will want to know what treatments are offered locally on the NHS and, if you wish to consider paying for private treatment, what private treatments are available locally. You should also find out if your GP will meet the costs of any prescribed drugs or if you will have to pay for them.

While GPs can do some preliminary investigations, you may need to be referred to a specialist fertility clinic. If so, you will need a referral letter from your GP. The provision of specialist services within the NHS is limited in some areas and waiting lists vary for certain types of treatment, so try and find out how long you will have to wait for an appointment.

Eligibility for NHS treatment

The type of treatment you can receive on the NHS depends on a number of factors, including what infertility services individual health authorities decide they will purchase.

Some patients will be investigated and treated only at their local district general hospital, others may be referred to a specialist unit. There is often a limit on the amount of treatment you can receive.

While most tests and investigations are carried out on the NHS, around 80 per cent of invitro fertilisation (IVF) treatment is carried out privately. You need to find out what the funding and selection criteria are to see if you will be eligible for NHS treatment. You could also contact the Human Fertilisation and Embryology Authority (HFEA – see 'Resources and Contacts' at the back of this book) for a copy of its *Patients' Guide* to clinics.

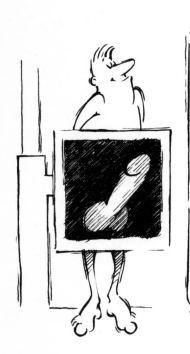

A specialist clinic will be able to carry out many different kinds of tests to see what the problem is and to find out which treatments will be best for you.

Clinics offer different types of treatment, and no single clinic is going to be best for everyone. Practical factors such as the opening times, the costs, the length of the clinic's waiting list and the travelling involved are also important.

The kind of tests that are done vary from clinic to clinic and all of the following may not be necessary as one or two may give a diagnosis. Once you have a diagnosis, fairly simple treatment or surgery may be all that is needed:

- Semen analysis to look at the number, shape and size of sperm and how well they move. More than one test should be carried out.

- Blood or urine tests to check hormone levels.

- Testing the sperm in special solutions.

- Special X-rays/scans to find blockages or check blood supply to the testes.

- Blood, urine and cervical mucus analysis to check hormone levels or ovulation.

- Ultrasound scans to check if a follicle, which should contain an egg, is being produced. Treatment for ovulation problems usually involves drugs by tablets, injections or nasal inhalations and has a high success rate if the correct diagnosis has been established.

- Sperm mucus crossover – this checks if the woman's cervical mucus allows her partner's sperm through.

- Endometrial biopsy – a tiny sample of womb lining (endometrium) is removed to check that it is free from infection and that ovulation has occurred.

- An hysterosalpingogram where dye is passed through the Fallopian tubes to check that they are open and clear of obstruction.

- A laparoscopy (usually under general anaesthetic) uses a thin telescope-like instrument to view the reproductive organs through a small cut below the navel. It checks for scar tissue, endometriosis, fibroids or any abnormality in the shape or position of the womb, ovaries or Fallopian tubes. At the same time a dye may be passed through the Fallopian tubes to see if they are open and clear.

Assisted conception

Where sperm counts are low or are absent, assisted conception may be effective. Assisted conception techniques have been used successfully for many years and a range of techniques are available. It is now possible for some men with very low sperm counts or even with no sperm in their semen to have their own genetic children. A specialist clinic will be able to advise you on which treatment will be best for you.

The most well-known treatment is invitro fertilisation (IVF) in which eggs are removed from the woman, fertilised in the laboratory and the embryo is then placed into her womb.

Donor insemination (DI) uses sperm from an anonymous donor when there are severe problems with the man's sperm. Gamete intra-Fallopian transfer (GIFT) uses a couple's own eggs and sperm, or that of donors, which are mixed together and placed in the woman's Fallopian tubes where they fertilise.

Intra-cytoplasmic sperm injection (ICSI) uses a single sperm injected into the woman's egg which is then transferred to the womb after fertilisation.

These are not miracle solutions. The age of your partner is very important and someone aged under thirty-five has a much better chance of a successful pregnancy than a woman over forty.

Donor insemination (DI) of sperm and donor eggs

If a man produces no or few normal sperm, carries an inherited disease, or has had a vasectomy, then insemination using sperm from an anonymous donor may be considered. Egg donation may be an option if a woman is not producing eggs or has a genetic problem. The decision to use donor sperm or eggs can be a difficult one. You can get help in making this decision from a counsellor or support group.

Clinics that offer this service have to send information about donors, recipients and the outcome of treatment to the HFEA. Donors have to meet extensive screening criteria, including HIV testing. A man may not usually donate sperm after ten live births have resulted from his semen donations. Donors do not have to be anonymous and most clinics will accept a donor that a couple has found for themselves.

Counselling and support

Couples report that the many hospital visits needed and the time spent waiting between treatments to learn if each stage has worked is stressful. All units providing IVF and other licensed conception techniques have a legal responsibility to offer counselling. Counselling can allow you to talk through what the treatment entails and how you feel about it, and can give support during the process and if the treatment fails.

If you don't want to see a counsellor at the clinic you are attending, the British Infertility Counselling Association can put you in touch with your nearest infertility counsellor (see Resources and Contacts). Some people find being in contact with others in a similar situation or with a support group helps them through infertility. You can contact CHILD (National Infertility Support Network) or ISSUE (National Fertility Association). See Resources and Contacts for details of your nearest one.

Self-help

There are some things you and your partner can do to help you be fit and healthy for pregnancy:

- Rubella infection in pregnancy can harm a developing baby so your partner should have a rubella (German measles) test to check if she is immune and if she needs a vaccination.

- All women planning a baby should take 400 micrograms (0.4mg) of folic acid every day from the time they stop using contraception until the twelfth week of pregnancy, as folic acid reduces the risk of a baby having neural tube defects, such as spina bifida. You can get folic acid from pharmacies.

- Men can improve their sperm by avoiding hot baths and broken sleep; by cutting down on alcohol, tea and coffee; and by taking garlic and selenium ACE supplement.

- Eat a balanced diet and try to eat five portions of fruit and vegetables a day. Don't eat too many foods that contain a lot of fat or sugar.

- Men should try not to drive for more than three hours a day. This has been shown to reduce male fertility because driving warms up the testes.

- Both try to give smoking up before as smoking is known to carry risks for the developing baby and also to newborn babies. This is important for men as smokers tend to produce fewer sperm and have more damaged sperm.

- You may need to reduce the amount of alcohol you drink – phone NHS Direct or ask your pharmacist for advice.

- Men should give up cannabis and other illegal drugs since these can affect fertility.

- Weight can affect the way your partner produces eggs – ovulation – so women who are very underweight or overweight might want to talk to NHS Direct or their practice nurse.

- Fertility problems in men and women can be due to sexually transmitted infections, particularly chlamydia or other forms of pelvic inflammatory disease (PID). These often produce no symptoms so either you or your partner could have an infection without knowing. If you are worried that you may have caught a sexually transmitted infection either recently or in the past, go to a genito-urinary medicine (GUM) clinic or sexual health clinic. The service is completely free and confidential. Most large hospitals have a GUM

> We both decided to quit smoking after two miscarriages. I was quite proud of us both until I caught him secretly smoking and blowing the smoke out of the cooker extractor fan.
>
> New mum

clinic and the Family Planning Association can tell you where your nearest one is.

In a 2000 survey by the Men's Health Forum and the Doctor Patient Partnership, 18 per cent of men surveyed thought a GUM clinic provided dental care.

On your marks
Antenatal care and pain relief

Your partner will be offered a choice of ways she can have antenatal care. This will be influenced by her previous pregnancies, medical health and social factors such as living in a remote part of the country which only the Australian flying doctor can get to in a rush. No matter what anyone tells you, being pregnant is not an illness and having babies may occasionally be a tad tricky but it is still normal and women have been doing it for a very long time. You do not need to 'go private'. There is no evidence that your baby or your partner is any safer than under NHS care. Private care might be more convenient but that's about it. All four of our kids are NHS babies, although I did deliver one myself which is cheating a bit, I suppose.

Hospital-based care

Women in their first pregnancy, where there is some reason to want closer observation or if a previous pregnancy was a bit hairy, are often advised to have full hospital care. Most women will have a named consultant and a named midwife who will take responsibility for your partner's checks as she approaches her delivery date. Antenatal regimes do, however, vary, and care may be provided, for example, by a community midwife. Parental classes are usually held in the maternity unit which is just great for ensuring as few men attend as possible. Pity, as they are great fun especially for us fat dads who empathise so much better. You are welcome to come along to these antenatal sessions especially for the first ultrasound scan. Never underestimate how scared your partner can be at that first session. A hot sweaty hand in her hotter sweatier hand helps more than you will know. It's easy to forget in that darkened room with the glowing totally incomprehensible screen that abnormalities are rare and all unusual positions in the womb can be safely dealt with. Now is not the time to mention that you get a better picture on Channel 5. Or maybe it is exactly the right time.

There are good alternatives to hospital antenatal classes, especially the classes run by the National Childbirth Trust (see Resources and Contacts).

> I have to say I found the antenatal classes intimidating. There didn't seem much point in the exercises but a midwife shouted at me, 'Come on, Dad. Get those tummy muscles in shape.' I never went back.
>
> New dad

Shared care

> The antenatal classes were brilliant. They had a video of childbirth. I nearly passed out then as well.
>
> New dad

Most GPs will offer a mix of checks at their surgery along with visits to the maternity hospital. Convenient and quick, it also ensures contact with a doctor who generally knows a lot about your partner's medical history. You can also attend these just like the hospital sessions. I have yet to find men beating a path to my door which is not surprising as most will only attend the surgery when they are in the terminal stages of a condition or when Liverpool FC are playing Manchester United mid-week.

Tests

There are routine checks made for simple things like anaemia, diabetes and blood groups but infections which can harm the baby are also checked with your partner's consent. HIV is not routinely tested for. Tricky one this. When AIDS first hit the scene people were pretty pessimistic about the whole thing. Not really surprising, it was the worst infection to ever hit modern people. Times change and so does treatment. Modern medicines have extended life span considerably. We know an awful lot more about pregnancy and HIV as well but it is useless if nobody knows whether HIV is involved. The British Medical Association Foundation for AIDS recommends getting tested but this is still controversial. Personally, I would sooner know if there is enough oil in the sump before the blue light comes on to tell me the engine is knackered.

Sickle cell disease in Afro-Caribbean people and thalassaemia in people with Mediterranean or Asian origins can affect babies even though there is no evidence of either condition in the parents. Tay-Sachs disease is also a risk when both partners are Jewish. Tests can predict the chances of this happening, allowing you to make decisions early on.

> The only thing I can remember is Bob telling me to hang on and that he loved me. I'm not sure I could have got through otherwise.
>
> New mum

Miscarriage

Spontaneous miscarriage is most common during the first three months of pregnancy. Relatives may mistakenly try to be positive with comments like 'there must have been something wrong with the baby' or 'you can always try again'. What is forgotten is that you and your partner are still grieving. While it is true that major abnormalities can lead to loss of the baby, we still know precious little about the process of abortion and why apparently perfectly normal pregnancies come to an early end. Suggesting to your partner that she may have produced an abnormal baby will not help for the next pregnancy. You should recognise her need to grieve and supply emotional support accordingly. Unfortunately, people may forget your own suffering. You too will be grieving but people may not realise that. There are

> Everyone made a fuss of my partner. It didn't seem to matter that I had lost our baby as well. When I told my doctor she told me it just was not the same for a man. She is probably right. I could have done with someone to sit and listen to me as well though, just the same.
>
> New father after a previous miscarriage

29

counsellors available for men as well as women and the maternity unit will put you in touch with them.

Signs of miscarriage

Recognising that something has gone wrong is not always easy and people can make mistakes in both directions. Any severe pain in the abdomen, particularly if it is associated with blood loss from the vagina, needs to be investigated. Many women report a lack of movement or just a 'feeling' that something is wrong. Many relatively minor conditions can mimic these symptoms. Urinary tract infections (cystitis) can often cause abdominal pain and even some blood in the urine. Even the pain of constipation has been mistaken for the onset of a miscarriage. In the case of a suspected miscarriage your partner needs to see a doctor. Generally she will be scanned by ultrasound (a painless and harmless examination using sound waves which pass though skin to produce a picture of the baby) and the baby examined for its well-being.

> When my partner lost the baby I was angry. With her, the doctors and myself. I didn't realise how badly it had upset me until I was in work and one of my mates joked about not being able to go out to the pub once the baby was born. They must have thought I was a right plonker when I started to cry.
>
> Man whose partner had three successive miscarriages. They went on to have a perfectly healthy daughter.

Fear of the unknown

Men might know precious little about their own bodies – ask the average guy where his prostate is and he'll scratch behind his ear which is three feet in the wrong direction to start off with – but knowledge of women's anatomy is restricted more or less to two areas. Which is handy as they are going to be the important bits for a while. Yes, women certainly need their brains and feet when kids come on the scene.

If you feel a tad apprehensive about childbirth, try to see it from your partner's point of view. If this is difficult, imagine pulling your top lip over your head while passing a rugby ball out of your bum. Now add some malicious bastard shouting 'push' right in your ear while a guy in a white coat with arms like a gorilla keeps checking to see if the ball needs a touch more air.

No matter how much women and men know about childbirth there is always the 'what if' factor to contend with. Pain is one of the greatest fears, for both partners. Bill Cosby was asked if there was a lot of pain during the birth of his first child. 'Man, it was terrible. She damn near squeezed the fingers right off me.' In truth, watching someone you love in severe pain is not easy to deal with and most men would gladly swap places, well after a couple of stiff whiskeys anyway.

There are choices of pain relief, from a complete absence of pain to no interference at all. Most important to remember and get through to your partner is that it will end. Most pain is endurable so long as there is definitely an end to it. It is made easier for your partner by having someone there whom they trust to tell them it is worth it, that something good will come from it, that there is an incredible thing happening which is far better to focus on than the pain.

Whatever path she chooses you can supply the distraction, cool towel on the head, back rubbing and most of all, encouragement. Some people say men don't belong at the delivery. Possibly, but it's up to you two not the midwife or doctor. It's your baby.

Alternatives to bullets, for the biting on

It is worth remembering that pain was once thought to be an essential part of childbirth and requests for relief considered to be less than godly. In 1591 it was considered a mortal sin to even ask for pain relief during childbirth as Eufane MacAyane discovered during the birth of twins in Edinburgh. She was promptly thrown into a pit and buried alive. We are more enlightened these days and nobody needs to be thrown into a pit although there are a couple of politicians I would like to volunteer.

Entonox (gas and air)

Great stuff this. Anaesthetists have been known to get too fond of their own gas. Your partner will have control over the amount of gas she breathes by holding the mask herself. It works best if inhaled just before each contraction so check yourself by keeping your hand on her bump and gently warning her to

31

start sucking as you feel the contractions start. Entonox is safe for both mum and baby but does tend to abolish any lady-like notions about bad language. Brace yourself for some toe-curling oaths. Some women hide under the covers on ward rounds as they remember what they called various members of the team including their partners. Entonox can also cause drowsiness and relaying instructions from the midwife or doctor is your job as she will often hear no one else's voice.

> When the contractions started I felt very alone, like going to the dentist without my mum.
>
> Single mum aged sixteen years

Pethidine

There are few pains this stuff won't touch, unfortunately it can only be used at certain stages of labour as it affects the baby's ability to breathe properly if given too late. An antidote is sometimes given to the baby if this happens. Pethidine can make you feel very sick, which is just marvellous. As if she didn't have enough to worry about at the other end. No matter how much noise she is making you don't need to shout. Keep your voice calm, she will still hear you.

Epidurals

Tiny amounts of anaesthetic injected around the lower part of the spine have a miraculous effect on pain during childbirth. Unfortunately it is difficult for the mum to sense what is happening and she must rely even more on the instructions from the team. It also makes her legs feel as though it's Friday night and they are totally incapable of walking.

Things you should know and expect with epidurals:

- They are safe but scary. Getting a needle stuck in your spine is not every woman's idea of a good day out and is faintly reminiscent of the film *The Matrix*.

- Your partner will be paralysed, not just pain-free, from the waist down. Ever woken up with a 'dead' arm? Same thing only you can wander around screaming you've had a stroke until someone points out that your legs seem to be working perfectly. Try rubbing and massaging her legs.

- An intense headache affects around 1 in 250 women and a sudden drop in blood pressure is fairly common. Your partner will feel faint and sick at first but it will pass. Lay on the reassurance by the bucketful. Comparing it to the last time you were out with the lads is not helpful.

- Sensation returns like the dreaded pins and needles of frozen hands. Massage her legs while she gives the cause of all this misery hugs and kisses. Yes, you are definitely number two for a while, mate, but it has its compensations.

There are other methods of pain relief including electrical blockage of pain signals (TENS) and hypnosis. Talk it through with someone who has tried them first.

Pressure is often put on dads by well-meaning staff to attend the birth. You and your partner should decide for yourselves whether you are there for the first bit, the whole job or none at all. Either way, it is an experience computer games have yet to match. Much, much more vitalising too.

Pleased to meet you
Tips on surviving the labour ward

LABOUR WARD

Despite welcome changes, there still lingers a whiff of exclusion for dads during childbirth. Labour wards are designed, obviously, for labouring women not expectant fathers.
Even though the mother must fast for sound medical reasons, it makes sense to have a partner who is not about to collapse from hunger during a long delivery. Education and preparation for the expectant father are both helpful and important but most of us have absolutely no idea of the emotional upheaval we are about to live through. Many men feel like a spare part yet the impact the presence of a partner can have on the confidence of a woman about to give birth cannot be understated.

When I was born, at home in Liverpool, my father, John Banks, had the job of fetching fresh bottles of Entonox (gas and air) and washing his son soon after being born. It was important to him that his role was clearly defined and he was able to play some part. When his grandson, John Banks, was born into the troubled world of Belfast, Northern Ireland, I did not have to ride a bike to fetch some Entonox. Just as well. The security forces took a dim view of men carrying large gas cylinders in the middle of the night. Men have a role to play, and with greater insight into the way a baby is born, a man can not only experience the miracle of birth but also make an invaluable contribution. This bit helps provide that insight.

> It's something you don't want to miss. It's better than just drinking and smoking.
>
> New father
>
> Actually, I would like to deliver the baby.
>
> Expectant father

Planning ahead

Plan ahead. Time off work is not yet guaranteed for a father in the UK. Early or late deliveries can put all the best-laid plans to nought. Two weeks past the 'expected date of delivery' is not unusual but can cause a disproportionate amount of confusion and worry.

Work out how you will get to the hospital. This is particularly important as labour can start at any time. If you do not have a car and cannot depend upon relatives or neighbours, call an ambulance explaining what is happening.

Signs of labour

Although most women are quite certain when labour has started, it is easy to mistake other things happening for the onset of labour. First pregnancies are a time for some confusion over contractions which may have little to do with labour. The uterus contracts about every fifteen to twenty minutes during pregnancy and these contractions last around twenty to thirty seconds. Such contractions are felt as a tightening around the abdomen. These 'Braxton Hicks' contractions become more frequent and stronger towards the end of pregnancy and can be confused with the onset of true labour.

If there is doubt you should ring your doctor or midwife

and be prepared to answer the following questions:

- How long have the contractions been present?
- At what intervals are they occurring?
- How long do they last?
- Has there been a 'show' (a watery, mucus discharge often tinged with blood from the vagina)?

> Every time she told me 'this is it' I nodded and carried on as we had been to the hospital three times already on false alarms. This time my partner told me this is really it and I could tell from her face that it was. It really was too and I was glad of all the 'dry runs' so I knew what I was doing.
>
> New father

If the labour is really taking place, the contractions will have been present for some time, even hours. Usually the interval between each contraction will be less than twenty minutes and the duration will be more than forty seconds.

Your partner should not eat before going into hospital, as the administration of a general anaesthetic, should it be needed, is very dangerous with food present in the stomach.

The real thing

Ritual still lives in childbirth, even in our supposedly advanced society. Thankfully we no longer shave the mother's pubic hair and fathers are welcome in most labour wards. But in ritual is a form of safety in familiarity. Breaking the ritual can be seen as 'bad luck'. Mercifully few of the rules of the labour ward have more to do with this form of protection than with sound clinical practice. Treating the father as a useless lump of dad, prone to trip over the drip or switch off the heart monitor instead of the TV, however, is a waste of a valuable resource. Having a job to do, such as masseur, water-bearer or a source of moral support, is infinitely better than wearing out the carpet in the waiting room. Worse still, dads can be ignored, as if they are some sort of wall hanging. Few men will have the pleasure of delivering their own child, but the support and love they give to their partner during childbirth is part of the bonding process which is often seen to apply only to the mother.

Machinery

There can be a baffling plethora of modern equipment in the labour ward. A great deal depends upon the type of pain relief being used and whether there are any potential problems that have been identified with the birth.

Foetal heart monitoring

The heartbeat of the baby is monitored throughout labour. The low tech method is to listen directly to the baby's heart with a simple form of stethoscope. Many men will have pre-empted this examination by the use of a cardboard liner from a toilet roll, which is a crude but effective way of listening to the baby.

This process can also be carried out electronically. One type of monitor is strapped to your partner's abdomen and senses the baby's heartbeat by ultrasound. The noise it produces has been used in many films, and once heard is seldom forgotten. It also tends to have an hypnotic effect on conversation, producing lengthy silences as the baby's heart slows and accelerates with each contraction.

Alternatively, an electrode can be clipped to the scalp of the baby which gives a more accurate picture of what is happening and is less prone to stop during a large contraction which just happens to be when you really want to know how the baby is getting on. The down side is your partner will be less mobile with all these contraptions attached. It is possible to do this through telemetry (rather like a radio microphone).

In some cases of distress where the heart of the baby is slowing and failing to recover quickly enough, blood may be taken from one of the small veins in the baby's scalp. It is an easy task to determine if there is sufficient oxygen present in the baby's blood or if it is being starved of its supply as it is being delivered.

I hadn't been to any of the antenatal classes with my partner, so I did not know what to expect when they took us to the labour ward. It looked like something out of *Star Wars*. I felt as though I was a total waste of space yet at the same time reassured that they could do something if anything went wrong.

New father

Stages of labour

Premature delivery can be postponed for a while using certain drugs, particularly if the baby is not yet developed enough to have a reasonable chance of survival. Most obstetricians would want the baby to be at least thirty-six weeks before labour begins, but some babies will survive even at an earlier stage.

The first stage

After the membrane which surrounds the baby ruptures it releases the liquid in which the baby floats. Breaking of the waters, as it is known, can produce a varying amount of fluid. Many women can confuse this with simply passing water, particularly if there are no contractions at the time. Usually, however, the membranes will not rupture until well into labour. This first stage of labour continues until the cervix, the neck of the womb, is fully dilated. During this time the position of the baby will be determined. This may involve an internal examination to check the progress of labour and to assess the position of the baby's head. Most babies are born head first, rather than in the breech, or head following, position.

> I felt useful. I talked to my partner – tried to take her mind off the pain. Told her stupid stories, told her the end justifies the means et cetera. I found it an intense hard graft but essential from my partner's point of view. I was proud of her because I knew she was terrified.
>
> Father of two children

The second stage

During the second stage of labour the baby's head appears, usually face down and rotates either way until facing to one or other side. Obviously it is important that this stage does not take too long but equally it has to be slow enough not to cause damage as the baby's head passes through the small confines of the birth canal in the pelvis. Your partner will want to push very hard at this point and it is important that you relay to her all the instructions from the midwife. You are aiming for a steady controlled appearance of the baby's head rather like the popping of a champagne cork. Simply talking to your partner and giving encouragement is enough, although a cool wet cloth on her forehead along with helping with the gas mixture makes her job a little easier. She may well use language that you never heard her say before and possibly

> I felt useless. When my wife was required to push, she was running out of energy and I could not help her.
>
> New father, baby delivered by Caesarean section

shout at the people trying to help. Importantly, many women say that the only voice they could hear during this stage of labour was that of their partner. It is easy to understand this given the effects of the pain, anxiety and any drugs administered to ease the pain.

The kindest cut of all

The man feels a mixture of worry for his partner and relief over the delivery. To prevent any severe tearing of the vagina, the midwife may perform an episiotomy which involves cutting the lower part of the vaginal wall as the baby's head is appearing. Local anaesthetic is always applied first but it still looks barbaric for your partner. Shortly after the birth the vaginal wall will be repaired by stitching. It helps if you are there to help maintain the distraction and provide support.

The third stage

The third stage of labour involves the passing of the afterbirth. It is a surprisingly large organ and is always examined carefully by the midwife to check that all of it has been passed. Mystery has always surrounded the placenta and probably with good reason. It is responsible for allowing the exchange of oxygen and waste gases between mother and baby. It allows the free passage of vital foods and vitamins but stops most pathogens, organisms which will harm the baby. Even the mother's own blood is not allowed to cross the placental barrier. The placenta sorts out what is needed by the baby and what is harmful. It is made up of a mixture of cells from the baby and those from the mother. When it is understood that the baby is actually a foreign body as far as the mother is concerned, and yet the baby is not normally attacked by the mother's defence system, it gives some insight into the sophistication of the placenta.

At times this balance is broken down and the baby is aborted by the mother's immune system. Similarly, the cells of the placenta may make an uncontrolled invasion of the mother and actually cause a rare form of cancer, now

> She told me she was sorry for swearing in front of all the hospital staff. They laughed when I said this to them. As far as I remember, my language was not repeatable either.
>
> New father

> My thoughts were elsewhere when the midwife told us she was going to make a small cut to help the baby out. My partner screamed and I felt it was all my fault that she was going through all this. Afterwards she explained why they have to do it. I didn't feel much better.
>
> New father

> I couldn't help but see the afterbirth. I thought, good God that's half her intestines. It didn't last long. I had too much to take in with a new baby crying, my partner looking at me as though we had just won the pools.
>
> New father

thankfully treatable. Primitive societies considered the placenta a powerful source of magic and would eat it. We are not a million miles away when you consider the so-called aphrodisiacs and longevity skin lotions which derive their 'potency' from various animals' placentas.

First impressions

Newly born babies are always short of air as they are born so they invariably appear blue. This is completely normal, as is the fine white cheesy substance (vernix) which covers their bodies. Most babies' faces look distorted along with their heads. Remember that the head has to mould itself in order to get through the narrow birth canal. A few good breaths, a quick rub and they actually look almost human. Not all babies cry when they are born, although it is encouraging if they do as it means they are expanding their lungs which have also been squeezed during birth. Both the squeezing and the crying help to get rid of the fluid which is always present in their lungs. Most adults, including men, on the other hand, weep unashamedly. Few men, no matter how big or tough, can resist this little bundle when handed to them.

Relief is usually the first emotion experienced by men after the birth of a baby, closely followed by awe at the presence of new life. Most men talk of their admiration for their partner, but it is difficult to put into words the emotion felt by any father at the birth of their child. Bonding is said to take place between baby and mother, but I suspect that a similar process takes place not only between father and baby but between man and woman. Furthermore, this extension of love encompasses much of the family, and is undiluted by the number of children a man may have.

People ask me did I cry, and I say, of course I bloody well cried, like a baby I cried.

New father

After our first child I thought I was pretty cool for the next baby. Sure enough, out pops our second baby and out comes the tears. I am the original macho man.

Father of two children

The unexpected

It would be dishonest to say that all deliveries go according to plan. Most problems like a breech birth where the bottom and not the head present first, however, can be predicted by good antenatal care including the use of ultrasound scans. Should a delivery pose a problem – if the second stage is too prolonged for instance – the baby may be assisted into the world. Forceps conjure up all kinds of misconceptions. Not only can they save the life of the child but they also avoid having to perform a Caesarean section. They are essentially a pair of scoops which fit around the baby's head. Using gentle pulling, the doctor can manoeuvre the baby through the birth canal without the mother having to push so hard. Despite all the old wives' tales it is very safe when performed by an expert, although it does look a little dramatic.

Ventouse cup is a vacuum-assisted delivery where a soft rubber cup is applied over the baby's head and a gentle suction applied which keeps the cup in place. The doctor can then manoeuvre the baby through its delivery. Both methods tend to cause some temporary distortion to the baby's head either from slight marks of the forceps particularly about the ears or a pronounced 'cap' on the baby's head from the vacuum delivery. Neither is permanent or dangerous. Again it is a balance of safety for the mother and child versus the discomfort of the assisted delivery. Supporting your partner is important and many doctors will not only allow you stay with your partner but prefer you do so.

> Each baby only increased my awe for my partner. How could she go through all of this even if it did give us such a wonderful family?
>
> Father of six children

> I said, 'Hello, I'm your dad.'
>
> New father

Caesarean section

One of the reasons why modern childbirth is so much safer for the mother is the speed at which the baby can be delivered by an operation should it prove impossible to allow a normal or forceps-assisted delivery. Placenta praevia, where the placenta is either over or very close to the opening of the womb, used to be invariably fatal for both mother and child as there was no way of detecting its presence until delivery. Such was the loss of blood as the placenta

> Living baby – relief and happiness beyond belief. Dead baby – devastation that I never even knew existed.
>
> New father of twins. He was present when it was discovered by ultrasound that one of the twins was dead while still in his partner's womb.

ruptured, along with the inability of the baby to be delivered past the placenta, that few survived. Thanks to ultrasound examination and Caesarean section, this is no longer the case.

Caesarean section can be performed under a general anaesthetic or by freezing the lower part of the body by injecting a local anaesthetic into the area around the lower spinal cord. This latter method allows the mother to see her baby as it is born and is pain free. You will usually be invited to sit with your partner as this is an experience which, like normal childbirth, can be usefully shared. Be reassured that you will be protected from the nuts and bolts of the operation, allowing you to concentrate on supporting your partner. You will be surprised at the informality of the event with every emphasis being made to allow you and your partner to enjoy your new baby. Most babies will spend a little time in an incubator after a Caesarean delivery as they can need a little more help keeping warm and getting enough air at the beginning.

> All the staff were in green, I was in blue, with a silly hat on. I couldn't have cared less, I just wanted it all to turn out right. I talked to my partner about the cat, the dog, anything. There was a green cloth separating us from the action. When the doctor said 'suction, please' I knew rightly so I looked over the cloth. There was our baby upside down. My partner asked if everything was OK. I said *he* was – sort of ruined the surprise, I suppose.
>
> Father of two children, the last born by Caesarean section

> I couldn't believe how informal the whole thing was. It was probably deliberate, to calm us down, but even I laughed when the surgeon said it was worse than fishing for a big pike.
>
> New father, baby born by Caesarean section

Scars can be more than skin deep

Most women worry about the scar the operation will leave and the effect it could have on any future attempts at having children by a normal delivery. For almost all Caesarean sections the scar will be very low down on the abdomen and runs sideways, not up and down, the abdomen. It is usually well covered by a pair of bikini bottoms and is often referred to as a 'bikini incision'. While some complications of pregnancy and delivery which require a section may make a normal delivery dangerous in the future, this is by no means true in all cases. It is your understanding of these points and help in the discussion which will reassure your partner when the day comes.

Incubators and jaundice

Seeing your baby in an incubator for the first time can be distressing, particularly for the mother. Such is the caution of modern medicine that the baby is given every assistance possible in the vital early hours and days of birth. In most cases it is a short-term aid, often in response to 'Apgar' scores which are lower than optimal. As the baby is born, the midwife or doctor will assess your baby for such things as muscle tone, the speed of breathing, heart rate and colour. This is checked again a short time afterwards and the results are combined as a score, or Apgar. Just because your baby is placed in an incubator does not mean there is a serious problem.

Temperature regulation is poor at the beginning and breathing may be laboured. An incubator supplies assistance for both. It is, however, a physical barrier and can inhibit the natural bonding which occurs particularly between mother and child. Most hospitals now encourage, whenever possible, the mother and father to handle the baby while in the incubator. Drips may also be used to supply fluid if your baby is having difficulty with breathing. This is particularly distressing for parents and I remember the shock of seeing an intravenous drip on our last child. Part of this came from having put so many up on babies myself years earlier.

If jaundice, which is also very common after delivery, should reach levels which might interfere with the baby's brain, ultraviolet lights are used to help break down the pigment which causes the coloration in the skin. Now that the blood type of the baby can be predicted and rhesus incompatibility be avoided, blood exchanges for 'blue babies', where the mother's immune system destroys the blood of the baby, are uncommon.

> My partner had everything worked out. She told me there was money on the mantelpiece – I thought she meant to tip the taxi driver with. When our daughter was born I had to ask the sister for a few bob to make the phone calls.
>
> New father

Aftercare

Most maternity units now favour having the mother up and about as soon as possible after delivery, even following a Caesarean section. Similarly mothers tend to go home much sooner than previously. For mothers this is a time of excitement and fulfilment, bringing home a new baby. Relatives and well-wishers will congregate en masse. Some will say, 'Well I know she has had a lot of visitors but I know she would want to see me.' There is a happy balance between having a few adoring people round and turning it into a circus. Gentle persuasion down the telephone advising a postponed visit can help.

Fear of the unknown

Death of a child during birth is not usually contemplated by the father to any great extent. Loss of their partner is even further from their minds. Such is power of modern expectation in contemporary medicine. More likely a dad will be worried about the pain and distress of their partner and the fear of a malformed baby.

Disappointment at the desired sex of the child will come after the confirmation of normality. This fear is highest for the first birth and worse after a child has been affected.

> I could not believe how much pain she was in. As the baby was being born I kept thinking, boy or girl, let it be healthy after all this.
>
> New father

When we lost a badly deformed baby, we were both counselled by a doctor who specialised in genetic malformation. I sat, unable to hear what he was saying for the waterfall of noise in my ears and the struggle to hold back a similar amount of tears. Fortunately he was a person who knew how pain and grief can limit the ability to concentrate. He drew a diagram which explained just how unlikely it was for this particular bolt of lightning to strike twice. As a dad, I had little doubt that it would all happen again. Our third child was finally born after what felt like a century. She had been tested for malformation by every test known to medical science. All the results were normal. I still did not believe them but it appeared to convince my partner that all was well. As our daughter made her debut to join her brother and sister I could hardly look, but had to in order to be able to answer my partner's demand to know was she all right! We had not been misled and a perfectly normal, beautiful child was ours. Only then did my partner open her hand and release the talisman she had kept through the whole pregnancy. A well-worn, creased piece of paper fell to the bedside. Through a waterfall of tears I could make out the chances of lightning striking twice in the same place.

Father of four children

Not until the last finger and toe is counted will a dad believe that everything is as it should be.

Hidden emotion

Being male has many advantages, not least that you are the one who only has to say push. It is not all on the plus side, however, and many men will find it difficult to cry in public. Holding a baby is natural, and men, despite their concern for dropping the new baby, catch on very quickly. It is rare for the man to have the first cuddle except following a Caesarean section by general anaesthetic. Watching men with hands used to lifting heavy weights or driving heavy machinery, gently holding and caressing their child which often fits in one palm is evidence enough of the potential bond which can, and often does develop between father and child. Yet despite the intimate contact, for many dads fatherhood starts nine months earlier with the positive home pregnancy test.

> Waiting nine months only increased my impatience to meet my son. 'Hello, mister,' I said, 'you took your time.'
>
> Father of six daughters and one son

Coping at home

Most hospitals insist on a midwife carrying your baby out to the car. This is not pure altruism. Your baby is the responsibility of the hospital until it leaves the premises. Weary dads falling down the maternity ward stairs, baby in arms, never looks good. A taxi is a good idea as well.

I never normally shout at other drivers, but on the way back home I found fault with every other car user. They all seemed to threaten us. My partner kept telling me to slow down, I could only have been doing 25 mph at the fastest!

New father

Your baby will have been seen, handled, admired and checked by everyone in the ward – doctors, midwives, relatives and possibly clergy. Now, at home, you have the baby to yourselves. It is a time of great peace, but short-lived. Soon you will have the relatives, well-wishers, neighbours and all the back-up services of modern medicine beating a path to your door. Investing in an answering machine which can give the time of birth, weight, sex, and hair colour (if any) of the baby is tempting. Be warned, people will want to know how your partner is, how the baby is, and did the baby cry when introduced to the world, before they ask about your crushed fingers and your role in the birth support team. Fathers, on the Richter scale of childbirth, feature low in the table of concern.

The worst part was worry over how I would cope – anxiety – sense of responsibility.

New father

The best part was a sense of completion, of achievement; an intense feeling of love and never, ever, being separated again.

New father

Other children

Having another competitor entering the pool is not always good news. Simply telling a child that from now on there will be another brother or sister in the house is the equivalent of informing a politician that a new candidate, younger and more attractive, has set up office in their backyard. Don't expect thanks. It is an unfortunate analogy, but there is the politicians' equivalent of the 'sweetener' when it comes to helping children accept the idea of an addition to the family. To simply expect them to welcome diluted attention from the most important people in their lives is wishful thinking. The average child can hate a newcomer to the family with a ferocity matched only by companies competing for the same contract. By showing attention to the older child, reassuring them that they are still loved and wanted just as much as ever, that their mummy and daddy brought along this new baby for them to play with is infinitely better than ignoring their feeling of insecurity. If a small present, in celebration of the event, happens to be one that the older child can play with along with the new addition, so what? You, your partner, and anyone within range will be invited to join in the celebration with food, drink and happiness, why not the one who feels they have the most to lose?

> Her older sister smiled a lot but the baby always cried when she was next to her. It was only when I found her little bruised ear did I realise what was going on. We gave her a doll which she promptly tore a leg off.
>
> Father of two girls

Depression

There is plenty of help available to parents. Your GP, community midwife, social worker and health visitor will all be sources of good advice and help. Naturally the new mum will feel exhausted and emotionally drained. For some this feeling not only fails to lift but can actually become worse and is called postnatal depression. Telling your partner to 'snap out of it' or to 'pull yourself together' is not only bound to make things worse but also increases strain on your relationship. Other children in the house will be quick to notice these changes and may interpret them as a sign that the new baby is not wanted. In severe cases, which are thankfully rare, your partner may need the attention of the family doctor. Postnatal depression is not the same as the common, some would call normal, phenomenon of the two-day baby blues. Weeping for no apparent reason is common for about two or three days after the baby is born. It rarely lasts more than a day or so but it helps to understand that nothing serious, other than emotional and hormonal changes, are involved.

> She became very serious, possessive and moody, attention-seeking. She blamed the kids for stealing the attention from me.
>
> Father who eventually divorced

Grieving

Relatives and friends are always unsure what they should do if a baby has a malformation or has died. Celebration, with empathy for the parents' grieving, is better than total silence when there is a problem with the baby. Talking about a club foot or Down's syndrome is better than simply trying to ignore it. All kinds of emotions will surface for the father to cope with, from his partner, himself and relatives. Unjustified feelings of guilt and shame are common. Many mothers feel as though a problem with the baby is their fault and they will look for possible causes. A fall, a recent stressful event, or alcohol taken during pregnancy will all be whips with which to beat herself. Fathers will also feel this self-guilt, but talking and reassuring is constructive, while taking part in the self-reproach is not. Rejection of you as a father is paradoxically not uncommon. If there is a problem with your baby of if your baby has died, it is very important to talk things through and expert help is available from your maternity unit. Support and advice is also provided by some of the the organisations listed at the end of the book.

> The baby was conceived while we had a few drinks. The health visitor said that alcohol can affect a developing child. I felt that it was all my fault for bringing the drink into the house in the first place.
>
> Father of child with special needs. Alcohol can effect a baby's development but in his case the cause was genetic. We have no idea just how risky it is to drink at the time of conception. I suspect, however, that a lot of families are started in this way.

Relationships

For many fathers, the homecoming is a conflict of emotions. Far from bringing fulfilment and a permanent party atmosphere, it can be major strain on a couple's relationship. Lack of sleep, uncertainty over the future and confusion over the division of affection all contribute to a feeling of 'unreality'. Many men will take off a few days from work to help their partner settle back home, despite the fact that there is a lamentable lack of parental leave for such occasions. Yet for some, if they are completely honest, it will be a relief to get back to work. Even so, returning to work when tired and trying to help at home with feeding and looking after the baby will also place a strain on your relationship. All those books and antenatal courses with their parent craft do not seem to apply to you and your baby. Only your baby cries for twenty-three hours per day, needs feeding seven times in the night and nobody else's partner treats them like a Martian. In truth, give or take the extraterrestrial reference, this is par for the course, but it gets better.

Returning to work is only the beginning. Work has not ceased when you leave your place of employment. Suddenly it is impossible to go out with friends; cinema and the theatre are fond memories. Even intimate moments with your partner can be interrupted or even take place in bed next to a babygrow which appears to contain a small octopus. Mixed feelings prevail. Self-fulfilment fights for supremacy with sadness over the loss of freedom. Like most things of any importance in a relationship, talking to your partner about your needs, the possible use of a babysitter, going out individually or simply staying at home and making it even more attractive is the best way of approaching this common dilemma.

Sex

There is no biological reason why you cannot resume intercourse as soon as both of you wish to do so. Common sense dictates that the presence of stitches, if an episiotomy has been repaired, will not make the experience something to look forward to, particularly by your partner. For some men there is a period of being 'turned off' by the whole experience. This is seldom a major problem and as things return to as near normal as they will ever be, given that there is someone else in the equation from now on, sexual relationships invariably improve. The same thing is obviously true for your partner and disregarding her feelings will only serve to put more strain on the relationship. As with sex during pregnancy, there can be ways of making sex more enjoyable, or even possible, after the birth of the baby. Different positions, a cushion under her hips or lying side by side may help. Lubricating gels can overcome the dryness of the vagina which may follow from the change in hormones. Libido you both enjoyed before the baby may not be the same afterwards but like swings and roundabouts, there are gains and losses. In the main, the losses are temporary while the gains are permanent.

Conception after childbirth

It is probably fair to say that most men are not considering another child immediately after the birth. And after what she has has just been through, it is probably the last thing your partner is considering.

There are some myths surrounding conception after childbirth:

- It is impossible to conceive until after the first period.

  Untrue, as many couples with closely spaced children will testify.

- It is impossible to conceive while breastfeeding, it is nature's natural contraceptive.

  Not true, on both counts.

- Your partner cannot take the pill until she stops breastfeeding.

  Not true. She may, however, be advised to change to the progesterone-only pill as the combined pill can affect her milk production while breastfeeding.

- Hormones in the pill will affect the baby, particularly if it is a boy, when breast-feeding.

  There is little evidence to suggest that these hormones harm the sex of the baby in the tiny quantities that are present in breast milk. Even so, some women may prefer to avoid any medicines or drugs during breastfeeding and use an alternative form of contraception.

> To some extent sex became less important, less frequent, more quiet.
>
> New father
>
> There was no real difference – maybe more loving, more sensitive.
>
> New father

Guilty relationships

For a number of fathers there is a flat emotional response to the baby after it arrives home. They can feel guilty that they are not continuously enraptured by their baby. Many fathers feel the real development in the relationship takes place when the child begins to respond or to smile in recognition. It appears that men crave recognition of their presence by the baby, particularly given the fact that this is more or less immediate for the mother. For some fathers, there is a link between a positive attitude towards the new baby and stable partnerships.

Positive memories of activities with their own fathers are also important. While this may seem obvious, if true it means that fathers who did not have such a good relationship with their own fathers may at first experience some difficulty in forming their own immediate relationships with the new baby. Even for these fathers, the recognition of their presence by their baby usually initiates a cascade of emotions which overcomes much of the initial inhibition.

Managing work and money

For many fathers, parenting is largely organised around work. In spite of the fact that more women are now in full- and part-time employment, fathers still earn two-thirds of family incomes. They also work the longest hours in the European Union. Such conditions make it incredibly difficult for dads to juggle work and family obligations. The situation isn't helped by inadequate parental and paterntity leave. In Britain men have the right to thirteen weeks parental leave, but unlike much of western Europe, this is unpaid, so most working fathers return to their jobs soon after the birth of their baby. Employers are currently under no obligation to provide paternity leave, though from April 2003 all dads will be entitled to two weeks paternity leave at £100 per week.

With babies costing in the region of £96 a week, the financial pressures are huge for many dads. Ironically, such pressures mean that many fathers in Britain end up spending more time at work after the birth of their baby than they did before. There is a greater demand in the home for money and concerns over finance can very easily cloud the enjoyment of a new child. Anxieties about money can be expressed in different ways such as apparent indifference, lack of patience and even excessive drinking which doesn't seem to stop after the initial celebrations of the birth of the baby.

Managing work, money and family is very difficult but there are practical things you can do in advance of the birth which will allow you to spend as much time as possible with your partner and new baby:

> It probably sounds very cold, but I actually was angry at him when he was first born for causing all the pain, for robbing me of my partner. But then he became aware of me and let me cuddle him and seemed to recognise that I was his dad. I feel terrible now about the way I felt, I hope there is nothing wrong with me.
>
> New father

> Probably my being a happier person made me more human, responsive, understanding, caring to those under my supervision.
>
> New father

> I did not work properly for a month. My whole life was affected and I am sure work was my last concern.
>
> New father

- Find out how much paid leave your employer offers and negotiate more if you can.

- Think ahead when asking for leave and offer your employer a strategy for dealing with any extra work or problems that will result from your absence.

- As soon as you know your partner is pregnant start saving for unpaid leave.

- Save up your annual leave.

- Be sensible about your workload – don't take on any new projects or major work committments.

In the first few months after the birth you are bound to feel exhausted, coping with baby, helping your partner and trying to keep up with work. The best advice I can give you is don't panic. Nearly all fathers feel like you and they get through it. My second piece of advice is don't expect too much of yourself. You just can't give 100 per cent at work right now, so cut yourself some slack. You can always make up for it later when things are a bit less hectic. Here are some ideas and suggestions for spending a bit more time at home:

> I am now doing the job of both partners (which I had to do when working) and enjoying it immensely.
>
> Divorced father

- Take your lunchbreaks at home, if possible. If not, can you work through your lunch hour so you can leave a bit earlier at the end of the day?

- Cut down on socialising after work.

- Try to start work earlier so you can go home earlier.

- Is there any way you can work at home more?

- Find out about job-shares and part-time work.

- Ask about voluntary reduced work time. Although this will mean a drop in salary, it can be minimal if you only take an afternoon off. It will mean that you can have a regular slot of time with your baby.

> My major fears were 1. the threat of redundancy and 2. if both mother and baby were healthy.
>
> New father
>
> Many fathers expressed the same level of anxiety over work and finance.

If you take the time to think about work and get organised before the birth, it will minimise the stress that is part and parcel of having a baby. It will also prevent tensions and arguments at home.

Attitudes towards breastfeeding

Where men have expressed concern or given reasons against breastfeeding they admit to:

- honest jealousy
  - less involvement with the baby if the father cannot give bottles
  - a desire to see the woman return to normal weight and energy
  - a revulsion for leaking and heavy breasts

There are no easy answers, and each of these reasons has its own built-in agenda which is the result of previous experience. While men harbour these concerns they often fail to discuss them with someone else, not least their own partner. Jealousy for attention is common and can be addressed by actually talking to each other. Not 'getting a look in' with regard to feeding the new baby is similarly a common emotion and can be expressed in ways apparently unconnected to the cause. Bad temper and lack of patience during feeding times are common manifestations of irritation. This can be overcome to some extent by allowing more cuddle time but also by bottle-feeding with expressed milk. This can have enormous benefits when the time comes for some intimate time alone and the baby can be looked after for a short time by a relative. Revulsion over the appearance and function of your partner's breasts is equally common and may even be of biological value, nature's way of protecting the food source for the baby. This revulsion can even extend to the vagina which, to some men, may never seem the same again.

Tactful discussion with your partner is better than innuendo, which leaves both of you wondering about your mutual attraction. Like the pain of childbirth itself, these changes have a finite duration. Such is the power of human sexual attraction, these feelings rarely become permanent obstacles to sexual relationships.

Male depression

Female baby blues and postnatal depression are very real

phenomena and have rightly received attention from both the medical profession and the media. But whereas society will sympathise with a woman suffering from, say, postnatal depression (PND), it is much more difficult for a man to admit to this problem. Few men would consult their GP and even fewer would ask for time off work and while we may be getting better at it, rather than analyse and discuss the problem, many men will demonstrate subtle, sometimes dramatic, changes in their normal routine. Drinking can be a serious attempt at consolation which seldom, if ever, gives even temporary relief. Men need to understand that like women they can suffer from a similar form of depression, that they are not alone with their ambivalence and that all around them, in the workplace, in the neighbourhood, there are other men with similar emotional needs.

> When my GP told me I had the 'baby blues' I just laughed, then I thought about it and got angry, but after a while I realised that she was right; it all started when the baby was born, or at least soon after.
>
> New father who eventually was prescribed a drug commonly used to treat postnatal depression in women. He is now completely back to normal.

Emotional burn out and its prevention

Burn out is probably a good term to describe what happens when a person gets an overload of responsibility, worry and fear for the safety of other people. This can happen to men who have become fathers. A major factor is not just the severity of the pressure but its perceived open-endedness. When such unremitting pressure is felt to be unending, people can rapidly become depressed. With the emotional trauma of childbirth, the lack of sleep, the financial implications and the impact having a baby has upon relationships with their partner, it is perhaps not surprising that many men can be affected.

> We only went for a drive into the country. But we were alone and it felt like being on holiday.
>
> Father of three, with a new baby

Even the most dedicated worker, teacher, artist, whatever, will admit to the need for a break, and parenthood is no exception. During the first two or three months it may be very difficult to find enough time between feeds to go out for an entire evening and it is important to organise some form of social support, for fathers as well as mothers. It is common for parents to think that they are the only ones feeling anxious and stressed, yet the arrival of the new baby brings together a whole range of people who have the same emotional strains and can support each other.

Adjustment

With some organisation, it is possible to work out a programme for time-sharing and there is an increasing number of fathers who are so deeply convinced that their role is equal to that of mothers that they take extended leave from work. In most parts of Europe there is legal provision to do just this. Sometimes this is for practical reasons, because the mother's salary is higher, or because the father is in an easier position to take a break from his work.

As this arrangement becomes more acceptable, fathers are expressing specific needs in coping with being at home. Like women, men can also be lonely at home and need emotional and practical support. All the dilemmas of isolation at home, lack of sufficient stimulus and the feeling of aimlessness are common complaints of men who may have anticipated few such problems. Obviously there is little difference here between men and women.

Baby problems

Traditionally, women have taken on the role of home doctor. Part of the reason why women present to their GP more often is the simple fact that they usually are responsible for bringing the children in when they are ill or for vaccinations. Most medical education is directed towards women and mothers, particularly regarding very young children and babies. Men as fathers were less likely to ask for medical advice. This had more to do with society's expectations and the perception of the male role than sound medical knowledge.

Objectivity can be difficult when you are suddenly responsible for the welfare of your child. While there is an army of people at the hospital, all dedicated to the health of your baby, at home you will be the link between your baby and this medical advice and help. Having knowledge is as important as being confident.

Did the baby scare you in any way?

Yes. I couldn't believe how dependent this little person was on such an ill-prepared parent.

New father

56

Small baby, big changes

Controlling your baby's temperature is particularly difficult, not least because of a baby's small body mass and relatively large surface area. Thus staying warm, or possibly more importantly, staying cool is not as easy as for an adult. During the settling period the baby may display all kinds of colour changes, spots, blotches, swellings and secretions. Thankfully, most of these changes are completely normal but can often look quite worrying. It is important to remember that when things do go wrong in a baby they tend to happen much faster than in an adult so if you are not sure about whether there is something really amiss, always give your doctor a call. They may not need to come out to you but you will be reassured.

> It came on quite quickly. One minute she was playing around then she started to vomit and became very listless. She was burning up and couldn't stand.
>
> Father of three children. His daughter, aged eighteen months, survived meningitis, probably because he brought out the doctor so swiftly.

There are a number of changes which never cease to alarm parents. It is helpful if you are aware of the more common conditions which can be mistaken for serious illness.

Head

Peculiar shape

All babies' heads are a strange shape when born. The skull bones are not completely joined together until eighteen months or so after the birth. This is to allow the baby's head to pass through the birth canal and in doing so the head is invariably squeezed out of shape. Marks from forceps, particularly around the ears, are common and rarely cause any problems for long. Similarly, if your baby was delivered using the Ventouse cup there may be a 'cap' over the head which is caused by the suction of the cup. It will disappear slowly without harm. Babies who have been looked after in an incubator for a number of weeks tend to develop long heads, flattened at the sides. This is also temporary and will gradually disappear as your baby is able to move the head more freely.

> When the doctor told me it was completely normal for the baby to have two holes in its skull, I felt an idiot, but my brother died from meningitis when he was a baby.
>
> New father

Soft spots in the skull (fontanelles)

As the baby's head has not finished growing and the bones of the skull are not all joined together, there are two soft spots on the skull which have no bone beneath the skin. Many parents are unnecessarily scared to even touch these areas. In fact there is a very tough, thick membrane protecting these gaps in the bone and it is highly unlikely that normal handling will cause any harm. They can be very useful for checking if the baby is dehydrated as they will sink down with lack of water. If they are ever very taut or raised like small mounds, you should call your doctor as it can be a sign of illness. They do tend to do this if the baby is crying very hard, but will subside when the baby calms down. If they remain taut or distended you should call your doctor (see 'Meningitis', p. 154).

Scurf on the scalp (cradle cap)

This is normal and is not caused by a lack of hygiene. A really thick cap-shaped layer is called cradle cap. Remove it by gently rubbing with olive oil. There are lotions available from the chemist under prescription but as cradle cap is not harmful it is best left alone and it will settle of its own accord (see 'Cradle Cap', p. 134).

> All the relatives were commenting on my son's blond hair. I am very dark, so I thought they were trying to say something, as it were.
>
> **Father of two**
>
> The boy eventually became quite dark-haired, but the way that genes express themselves is complex and babies can show little resemblance to either parent.

Hair

There is a great deal of ignorance and superstition over hair on a baby. In fact, any amount of hair on the head, from baldness to long flowing hair which reaches down the back, is normal. Extra time spent in the womb, say a couple of weeks, can often result in more hair. Most of the hair will be lost soon after birth anyway.

Eyes

No matter what colour your or your partner's eyes happen to be, most babies' eyes are blue at birth and change gradually to their permanent colour. Thankfully, the serious eye problems which were once associated with childbirth and are still seen in many underdeveloped countries are now very uncommon in the UK.

Crusting on lids and lashes

Sometimes this can be yellow and may even stick the lids together. This is the result of a very common mild infection known as sticky eye. It is not serious but the baby should be seen by the doctor who will recommend drops or a solution for bathing the eyes. Remove the crust using cotton wool soaked in water or saline (see 'Conjunctivitis', p. 129).

Wandering eye

An eye which appears to have a mind of its own and wanders about, particularly when the baby is looking intently at something close up, is in most cases completely normal. If this persists, or if your baby can never appear to focus both eyes at the same time on an object, you should inform your doctor or health visitor.

Skin

A new baby's skin is delicious to kiss. It has a fragrance and softness which must have some effect on the adult smell and brain and enhances the protective instinct. Unfortunately their skin is easily damaged by their own urine, causing a nappy rash, and tight clothing or nappies can tear the skin. Loose clothing, which presents no danger of suffocation, along with changing nappies before the skin reddens will avoid most of these problems (see 'Nappy Rash', p. 163). New babies can also demonstrate an almost chameleon-like change of colour which can be alarming to watch yet rarely has any significance.

Spots and patches

The most common type of spot seen on new babies are red spots with yellow centres called neonatal urticaria. A big word for a small baby. These spots form because the baby's skin and its pores do not yet work efficiently. No treatment is required and they will invariably disappear after the first couple of weeks. 'Spots' which look like bruises and do not turn white when you run your nail over them, especially if the baby is crying, off feeds, hot, or irritable, should be reported to your doctor as some forms of meningitis present in this fashion. Generally speaking, however, if the baby is feeding, appears happy and is not crying, is not increasingly drowsy and has a normal temperature, a spot does not mean a lot.

Ears

Wax and smelly discharge

All babies will have wax in their ears. While it is reasonable to remove any wax which appears at the very outside of the ear, trying to remove wax from within the ear will only result in packing the wax in tighter and irritate the ear canal such that it will produce even more wax. A smelly discharge, often yellow in colour, particularly if the baby is irritable, may indicate an infection. Your doctor can advise (see 'Middle Ear Infection', p. 161).

Abdomen

Swelling

Many babies will have a swelling just around the navel. It will be more pronounced when they cry or pass a motion. It is caused by a weakness in the muscle in the area of the navel which originally allowed blood to flow through the umbilical cord. It is called an 'umbilical hernia' and most such hernias right themselves completely by one year. Very few ever need surgery, but if required it is a very simple operation performed when the child is a bit older. If your baby has a permanently distended abdomen, particularly if they are not passing any motions and are vomiting repeatedly, you should inform your doctor (see 'Crying Baby', p. 137).

Vomiting

Posseting of a little milk after feeds is normal. Repeated vomiting, particularly if the vomiting is so violent that the vomit travels a half metre or so (projectile vomiting), needs the attention of your doctor as there could be an obstruction in the stomach or bowel. Fortunately such obstructions are now readily treatable by a relatively simple operation (see 'Vomiting in Babies', p. 178).

Crying and sleeping

The only way a baby can communicate to you that they are not happy is by crying. It may not be the most informative way of telling you what they want but there is usually a pattern in the cry which most mothers, and increasingly fathers, can interpret as being either minor, important or requiring urgent action. Generally speaking, if it is possible to distract them with a cuddle or play, then it is not serious. If they continue to cry despite your very best attempts with aeroplanes, trains, noises from the jungle and old-fashioned cuddles, then it may be because of:

> It never ceases to amaze me how such a small bottle of milk looks so much when it comes back up again
>
> New father

Dirty nappy

Never underestimate the effect of urine in contact with raw skin. A child who cries and then stops when the nappy has been changed has given you their verdict (see 'Nappy Rash', p. 163).

Lack of food

Hunger is a powerful stimulus for a baby to cry. How else will it make clear that it is time to feed? Nature has ensured that this type of cry is particularly piercing, persistent and difficult to ignore. Small bodies need small amounts of food regularly. Night is the same as day to a small stomach. Babies who continue to cry even when being fed are trying to tell you something. Feeding is a natural analgesic and comforter, but if the real cause of the crying is not hunger, and if your baby is not settled by feeding, look for another possible cause (see 'Feeding', p. 76).

Windy stomach or colic

A build-up of gas in the bowel, which is common when your sole source of food is milk, can cause pressure on the bowel and thus pain. It will also stop you from taking any more food even though you are hungry. Net result, a spasmodic cry which is often relieved by simply changing the position of the baby with gentle tapping. A sudden release of pressure from either end, followed by a cessation of crying, gives you your answer. There are medications available for babies who are particularly prone to wind and colic, but as most cases of wind and colic are self-limiting, they are best avoided until all the simple, time-honoured methods such as rhythmic movement have been tried and exhausted – like yourself (see 'Abdominal Pain', p. 108; and 'Colic', p. 128).

Hot, cold, lonely, sleepy, fed up . . .

> I would talk to him, tell him stories, sing to him, play with him until my wife would say 'that's enough, let him go to sleep now'.
>
> Father of two

As a baby cannot move to somewhere better, they can only cry to make things better for themselves. If they are too hot, cold or fed up with staring at the same ceiling for two hours, they may cry. Similarly, and paradoxically, if they are sleepy they may also cry. Recognising the pattern of the cry is important, but at the end of the day, and it usually is, you may not be able to identify just what is really wrong other than that it is nothing serious. Although the majority of babies do not cry continuously, crying can cause considerable exhaustion in parents. This may cause friction in your relationship, particularly as men still do not have the legal right to remain at home during this exciting but demanding period. Some babies cry more than others, even within the same family. After trying all the stand-bys, soothers, rocking, music, singing and dancing, you need to take a break. If there is obviously nothing serious, step back for a while. It will not hurt to let your baby cry on for a few minutes while you have a cup of tea and rest. Taking turns between you and your partner will help give each other a break. Often your return and a fresh approach will do the trick. Talking to others about it can also help. You may be surprised at how many people have lived through the same experience. The name of the game is to pace yourself. An exhausted father with an exhausted baby is not a good combination. Spread the load if possible.

> What were the three worst things about having a new baby in the house? 'Lack of sleep, lack of sleep and lack of sleep, in that order'.
>
> New father

If there is a change in pattern of your baby's cry, either in duration, nature or sound, it may mean there is a problem. Every now and then check that none of the other causes of crying have returned to prolong the agony. Keep your mind open to a real problem if your baby never normally cries in this way (see 'Crying Baby', p. 137).

Bedtime

For very young babies the 24-hour day is broken up into periods of sleep, wakefulness and feeding. Night-time is not yet a concept to which they have become fully accustomed. Some babies will sleep longer than others. Similarly, some babies will feed longer than others. You will find ways of improving the sleep pattern of your baby. For instance, an absolutely quiet house may well help to maintain their sleep, but as this is almost impossible, it is a good idea to get them accustomed to ordinary household noise while they sleep. A warm bath or feed just before putting them to bed can also help (see 'Cot Death', p. 131).

Our first baby slept in our bedroom. I was up and about with my wife every time the baby opened his eyes.

Father of two children

I'm a light sleeper and each noise he made woke me up for months. In macho style I'd do the middle-of-the-night feeds and sometimes he wouldn't go back to sleep. With an incipient hangover this was hell!

Father of three

Lack of sleep

Sleep deprivation is a well-recognised form of torture. It can disrupt your normal life and your relationship with your partner and sour the enjoyment a new baby should bring. If possible, share the load. It is desirable to allow your partner to nap during the day if she is breastfeeding. Bottle-feeding, whether from expressed milk or concentrate, will allow you to take part of the responsibility for night feeds.

Even in a mind-fogged, sleep-deprived fugue it helps to know that this period of mixed torment with pleasure will not last so long. Until the next child comes along, that is. Strangely, you tend to forget the bad bits and remember only the feeling of peace and exhilaration of holding a new baby, when the decision whether or not to increase the size of the family comes around.

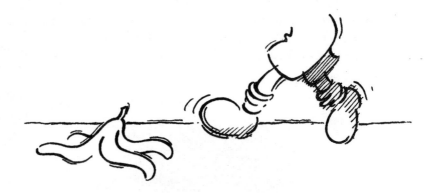

Accidents to children

Most injuries happen in the home with children up to age five. They can happen very quickly and are more likely when adults are under stress, in a rush or when their usual routine is changed. Because you know your own home, you are in the best position to look out for possible dangers.

The kinds of accidents children have are related to their age or level of development so there are particular things to watch out for depending on the age of your child.

Babies: 0–1 year old

At this stage babies are able to wriggle, grasp, suck and roll over. There are a number of possible accidents that are common in this age group.

Suffocation and choking

Babies can swallow, inhale or choke on items such as small toys, peanuts and marbles, so ensure these things are kept out of reach. Choose toys appropriate to the age of your baby and encourage older children to keep their toys away from your baby. Avoid pillows and soft bedding. Do not put infants to sleep unattended in an adult bed or on the sofa.

Falls

These are particularly likely if you leave your baby on a raised surface. Be sure, when you are changing nappies, that you avoid the possibility of the baby rolling off a bed or sofa. You can use a baby mat on the floor. This also applies when you use changing rooms in supermarkets and when attaching baby restraints.

Burns and scalds

Avoid placing your baby next to hot or warm objects such as ovens, light bulbs, radiators, curling tongs, hairdryers, irons and fires. Place hot drinks out of reach. Fit short power leads on kettles and heaters. Remember, hot water can still scald up to thirty minutes after it has boiled.

Poisoning

Babies' natural instincts are to suck anything which comes into contact with their mouths. Many ordinary household substances can be poisonous. All poisonous substances should be kept outside your baby's reach at all times.

Care should also be taken when washing babies' bottles, so that they do not come into contact with poisonous substances. Young brothers or sisters should be supervised when around babies to stop them feeding tablets or other poisonous substances to the baby – 'Taste this, little bro.' Remember, babies' stomachs are much more sensitive than adults'.

Children: 1–4 years old

Toddlers can move very quickly so accidents often happen in

seconds. As children get older they will explore more, which means they are more likely to receive knocks and bruises, not least from their adoring brothers and sisters. Blinking while they are this age is a hazard.

Falls

Small children can squeeze their bodies through a gap as small as 10 centimetres wide – smaller than the length of a teaspoon – but they may get their heads trapped. Check the width between railings, banisters and balconies and board them up if necessary. Fit window locks or safety catches that stop windows opening wider than 10 centimetres.

- Move furniture such as beds, sofas and chairs away from windows to prevent children climbing up and falling out.

- Fit a safety gate at the bottom and top of the stairs. Use a safety gate to keep small children out of the kitchen too. Make sure older children know they should keep the gate locked. Thankfully not that many kids turn up in casualty with pots stuck on their heads.

Burns and scalds

Make sure you use an appropriate fireguard for all fires. Fit a smoke alarm on each floor of your home and check that it is working properly on a weekly basis. It is a good idea to have a fire escape plan worked out and to tell your children what to do in case of a fire. My dad used to stand in the bedroom and shout, 'This is not an fire drill it's an I'm-coming-to-get-you drill.' Life was easier then as we lived in a single-storey prefab and a fire would have helped dry the paper walls out a bit.

- Place hot drinks out of children's reach and fit short power leads on kettles and heaters. Use the rear rings of the cooker, keeping pan handles turned away from the edge. Children are curious and will reach for handles of pans on the stove.

Poisoning

At eighteen months or earlier children can open containers and by three years they may also be able to open child-resistant tops within minutes.

- Keep household chemicals, medicines, alcohol and even cosmetics out of children's reach, preferably in a locked cupboard or lockable suitcase or cosmetics case.

Tired of warning him about using cola bottles for storing weedkiller, one woman gave her husband a drink of cola when he came in thirsty from work. 'Agh,' she screamed, 'I've used the wrong bottle.' He immediately ran to the tap, drank half a gallon of water followed by a few large mouthfuls of soil from the back garden. Only after his third mouthful did she tell him she only meant it was diet instead of regular cola. Marriages survive that sort of shock every now and again but then so do kids.

Getting to know you
Superglue bonding and plain talking

Mum's the word. It certainly is if you are three weeks old and breast-fed. Dads are people who give great hugs but are a bit short on the goodies. Babies have little contact with their father in the early days and awareness that there are two important people in their lives arrives slowly with time. Dads are usually waiting in the wings. Children become aware of their fathers gradually and some dads do the same thing with regard to their new baby.

It is a reflection of just how powerful a simple show of affection can be that as the child grows they are prepared, occasionally, to leave the arms of their source of food, their breastfeeding mother, for those of their father. All of ours, however, did a quick check to make sure Mum hadn't nipped off permanently, before chewing contentedly on my nose. Cuddle quality is important. In experiments on animal behaviour, baby chimps will favour a warm, hairy dummy with no milk to a cold, smooth dummy mother supply. The chimps spent their time between both, using the non-hairy dummy simply as a supply of food.

Being a fairly tense sort of person, I was a mug for all the stress toys which you squeeze, punch or otherwise abuse to let off steam. When my daughter came along, I found the perfect stress release. A cuddle always did the trick. I'm sure she has stopped me having a heart attack!

New father. Having something to cuddle, even a cat or dog, prolongs life. This is supported by statistics which show that men in stable relationships who have children live longer on average than single men with no children.

Talking

Give the average man a three-week-old baby and all the efforts of parents and teachers to convey good English goes out with the nappy liner. It's not surprising that so much of language is rendered obsolete. Most men say their relationship with their child really takes off once they start talking.

Talking, if we mean communication, actually takes place very soon after birth. Babies indicate what they want very effectively by using their voice. Mothers can tell the often subtle difference between cries, from the demand for food to that of wanting attention. Fathers are also able to do so, but usually later on.

Conversation also takes place. Inflections in voice, along with the urgency with which it is spoken by the baby, convey a great deal of information. Some babies respond to loud talking, others to soft gentle speech. This may reflect the amount of background noise in the home but may also be an expression of

69

> I communicated through lots of touch, caresses, kisses, hugs, whispers, words and sounds which weren't words.
>
> Father of three

their own personality. From this type of contact we very quickly learn what babies like in the style of conversation. Admittedly much of the conversation is one-way.

Opinion changes between generations on the style which should be used when speaking to a baby. Modernists reject baby talk and insist that we speak to children as miniature adults. Traditionalists say this is useless and robs the child of the intimacy of such talk. Speech of whatever form which maintains a constant pitch does not have the same attraction to babies. Rhetoric is probably appreciated at a very early age and as all politicians know well, on occasion it is not what you say that counts, but how you say it.

All babies probably hear a mixture of baby talk and everyday words as they are constantly picking up conversation not directed to themselves. Children suddenly repeat a phrase or word which most certainly would not have been for their ears. With exquisite timing, they will always wait until they are in the most genteel company of adoring aunts before making these utterances. Babies adore repetition, especially in speech. Telling or singing the same nursery rhyme may be boring to you but to your baby it is a recognisable pattern in an otherwise chaotic world. Even as they grow older the desire for repeatability remains and reading the same story over again becomes par for the course. Children will allow a certain amount of variation on the theme but the basic structure has to remain the same. It is the gentle nuances in speech which introduce variation. Not a million miles away from constantly sung football or rugby songs, adult men find security in the predictable chant as do their children. It is the group involvement which supplies the confidence. Singing a nursery rhyme for the hundredth time conveys commitment and security. Variation is the name of the game, so long as it is within certain boundaries of familiarity.

> But Dad, I was the one who got the coconuts from the tree. John killed the monster crab. I wish you could get it right.
>
> Beth, six-year-old daughter of author, on bedtime stories

Catch-22

Babies are already exposed to their mother's speech while in the womb. This is reinforced by intimate contact after being born. Babies are often little disturbed by a mother's sneeze or cough. There exists for men, therefore, a catch-22. Men have not only traditionally been slow to talk to their babies, possibly through self-consciousness, but they have had less opportunity to do so. Many men leave for work while their children are in bed and return from work to find them in the same place. For all these reasons, and more besides, the baby learns and becomes accustomed to Dad's voice after Mum's. Get your face in there as well. If your baby can't recognise your mugshot they will cry, which just puts you off trying in the first place. Make sure too that you spend time on your own with your baby as soon as possible after the birth. This is crucial for developing a relationship with your child and will help to build your confidence.

> When I went out to work they were in bed. When I came home they had already gone to bed. I used to sit in the dark and talk to them as if they were awake. My daughter told me how sorry she was about the factory cat being run over. As far as I remember, she was fast asleep when I let that one slip.
>
> Father of three, shift worker

Brain pain

Frustration is written all over the face of a child who can understand speech but whose brain has not yet worked out how to actually speak. A similar but more devastating phenomenon occurs with the adult brain which has been damaged by a stroke. A common result of such injury is the ability of the person to recognise an object but be unable to state its name. A watch becomes 'time' or 'day'. Such is the frustration they will often substitute a string of expletives which can be startling in their clarity compared to the hesitant inaccurate speech of which they are normally capable. Babies and toddlers are just as frustrated and will become impatient when you fail to understand that the unintelligible collection of consonants they are hurling at you at top volume simply means 'I want a biscuit.' Interestingly, they will often treat the adult as an idiot and turn to one of their older siblings to act as an interpreter who promptly says, with just a touch of superiority, 'He wants a biscuit Daddy.' When all else fails on the language front, babies will simply point a finger until you get it right. This can lead to a crescendo of frustration both from the baby, who patently considers the father an idiot, and the father who simply feels like an idiot. Part of the pleasure of

> I used to sing 'Goodbyee' and carry him around the house and talk about shapes and sights.
>
> Father of three

fatherhood is getting the pointing finger correct and guessing what the baby wants. Like many facets of parenthood it is usually short-lived as your baby recognises a way of maintaining attention even when there is no immediate object of desire. The pointing finger is truly a powerful tool in learning the name of things and keeping you there.

Helping them to talk

> You missed a page, Daddy. You missed one last night too only I didn't tell you.
>
> John, son of author, aged three

A child's ability to experiment with words and language is vital for coping with many other facets of learning later on in their development. Some dads find talking to a baby very difficult. Often these dads will also find small talk difficult, and would prefer to say nothing rather than talk just for the sake of it. If you are like this, and you are in the majority of dads, look for opportunities to chat.

Dressing and feeding

Babies and toddlers are fascinated by clothes. It helps if you talk them through all the various bits when you are dressing and undressing them. Babygrows can produce a most stimulating conversation, as there always appears to be one press-stud too many. Now is the time to practise expletive-free conversation. Feeding is a similar opportunity for conversation. You won't be the first father to explain that the rapidly approaching spoonful of baby food is in fact a train about to enter a tunnel.

Picture books

A time-honoured way of promoting interaction. You supply the commentary and pointing finger, they supply the laughs and impatience to see the next page even though you are only halfway through this one. Don't underestimate what is going on during these sessions. Many a baby will let you know very quickly if you have turned the page before they have digested the previous one completely. Memory in a young child is uncluttered with telephone numbers, useless facts and dates. They have plenty of room, therefore, for what you said the last time you went through a particular story. Going too fast and skipping large chunks will be noticed by your child who will not be slow to let you know what they think of the room service.

Question time

Conversations should be two-way. Asking questions like 'Did you like that?' may not produce definitive answers but you may be rewarded by a gleeful shout. Remember to answer their questions as well. They may not sound like questions but any response is better than none. Avoid answering your own questions too often and allow them time to make their verbal or non-verbal response.

Milestones of development

Being involved as a father is not only important to your child, it is important for your memories of how they grew up. Part of the fun comes from listening out for the stages of language development. Listening to a child experiment with words raises apprehension over the speed of their development. Medical textbooks will lay down milestones through which the child should pass during normal development. These indicators of 'normal' development can be a source of constant worry for the parents of completely normal children who fail to meet the deadline on time. Failure to build a tower of four bricks can be endured but a failure to talk is often seen as a real disaster and portends failure in society. If these books are read carefully they will explain that 'normality' is not only impossible to define but that it is also undesirable when talking about human beings of whatever age. Most doctors happily settle for the average age at which a milestone will be reached with the sure knowledge that there will be children who are a little above or below this average yet who will be as 'normal' as the next child. Teachers and health visitors are probably better people to talk to than doctors and they will agree with the

> As each week passed and she still lisped her Rs, I grew more despondent about her future speech. Some time after, I attended her school open day. All her essays were pinned onto the classroom wall, complete with gold stars. They were marvellous, full of adjectives and description.
>
> Father of three

medical profession that children have different rates of development in different areas. One of our children was slow to perfect her speech and was borderline for help from a speech therapist. More importantly, however, she could experiment with language and would use it to produce the greatest response for her demands rather than praise for grammatical correctness. Your health visitor can check on your child's speed of development.

> With five children it was easy to see a pattern. Our eldest started speaking first, and with each successive child the delay got greater. They were finding that they did not have to use spoken language to communicate what they wanted.
>
> Father of five. This is not always the way for all children. For some the stimulus of other children talking seems to trigger their own use of speech.

Bite your tongue

Allow some mistakes in their speech. Constant correction will impede experimentation. Nursery rhymes, songs and chants are all good ways of instilling confidence with language in a child and they do not need to be in BBC English. Patience and encouragement will pay great dividends when your child first tries to tell a story, and will allow them to develop their expression through language. Energetic use of language to get a message across, which is why it was invented in the first place, is more important in the early stages than its grammatical accuracy. Exactly when they start is less important than how. If a child can get by with expressions and body language easily interpreted by their brothers or sisters, it may reduce the stimulus for talking. Alternatively, the intimate and often sustained contact with their brothers and sisters who are talking increases the exposure to speech. All our children began to speak at different times and it had little if any effect on their ability at school.

> Coming home tired, the last thing I want to do is play wrestling on the carpet. Yet once it starts I feel refreshed. Perhaps it is just so different from my daily grind at the desk.
>
> Father of one

Play

Play is the great leveller, bringing both baby and father onto the same plane of simply having fun. Without a doubt there may be a conscious or unconscious attempt to teach and learn, but for a brief spell baby and father are united in warmth and need no language. Given that play appears to have constructive value, it tends to be delegated to people who have more free time. This is the equivalent of growing a prize melon but letting someone else eat it. Play is a learning experience. It not only develops ability at art or construction, it also builds confidence, promotes sharing and even allows children to teach other children without them realising what they are doing. More important for fathers, it is a tax-free way of letting off steam, doing something just because it is fun. Paradoxically, play with your child can be hard work. Even so there are ways of limiting the effort and increasing the pleasure.

Stories and plays

Children love stories and plays. It is part of getting ready for real life. They particularly like to act out what they hear and make up. Puppets, and these can be as simple as socks or ice lolly sticks tied together, provide a material basis for their imagination. Older children tend to direct. Like the younger ones, you should be content to supply ideas and play the bad guy.

Storytelling need not be straight from a book. Develop a theme such as 'islands to be shipwrecked on', or 'tunnels that lead to . . . You need only provide the canvas, they will supply the paint. Imagination is more powerful than any printer's ink.

Painting

Painting comes naturally when young. Unfortunately young people tend to paint everything except the paper. Getting upset over the mess is about as useful as Kanute opposing the next tide. Invest in a large sheet of plastic floor covering and packs of brushes, paint and child-safe felt-tip pens. Avoid invoking rules for play with very young children. They will develop their own rules, which like politicians' oaths, tend to be flexible.

Our table invariably ends up like a Salvador Dali creation. Polyurethane varnish is truly a wonderful invention!

Father of five

Strongman act

Dads are perceived, rightly or wrongly, as being stronger and you will often get away with more rough play than your partner. Allowing them to ride around on your foot, having slipped all the way down from your chest, may not be particularly comfortable, but it is awesome to a child and probably stops your blood vessels furring up.

Feeding

Eating is not the same as feeding. Babies feed, they do not eat. This is not to say they do not appreciate good taste. What defines good taste to a baby may have a great deal to do with texture. The difference has nothing to do with what is eaten, but rather, how it is eaten. Babies approach this by the two steps forward, one step back method. If bottle-feeding, it is important to follow the instructions on the tin very carefully. It is not simply because of the amount which may or may not be taken, although this is important to make sure the baby has enough food, but also to maintain the dilution of the food with water. If it is too concentrated the baby will become constipated and may even become dehydrated; too dilute and the baby will be constantly hungry and will pass very loose motions.

Great care is needed when using a microwave for heating bottles. It cannot be a substitute for sterilising them in the first place. Microwaves can also produce localised hot spots in the milk and even within the plastic of the bottle itself. They should be avoided unless there is absolutely no other way of warming the bottle.

Hygiene

Gastroenteritis is uncommon in breast-fed babies. Very young babies rely to a large extent upon the natural defences against infection passed on from the mother during pregnancy and from breast milk. Bottles and teats, therefore, need to be kept as clean as possible by the use of sterilising agents. Every father will find his own method of feeding which works for him. Some form of gentle distraction such as rocking or background music can help. I personally exhausted my entire memory of Beatles songs which, along with a bit of rock and roll, seemed to do the trick. Vomiting comes with the feeding. It is normal for the baby to bring up a fair proportion of what went down. Better to place a clean towel under your baby which will collect the semi-digested milk than a plastic sheet which means you will be cleaning the carpet instead.

Warning signs

Failure to feed or irritation during feeding should send off alarm bells. Babies have a very limited reserve of fluid and will dehydrate quickly if they are vomiting repeatedly or have profuse diarrhoea. Skin which remains puckered when gently pinched between thumb and finger can be a sign of dehydration. Repeated vomiting, particularly if followed by a demand for more food, may be a sign of a very treatable condition called pyloric stenosis. It involves a progressive narrowing of the opening of the stomach and is characterised by repeated vomiting in the very young baby. This type of vomiting is hard to miss as it is highly projectile and will travel a metre or so across the floor. Babies with this condition rapidly lose weight but with early recognition of the problem will rarely come to any harm.

> I had heard of projectile vomiting from a television programme. Believe me, the word projectile suits very well.
>
> Father with a new baby who developed pyloric stenosis which was successfully treated by surgery. There have been no further problems.

Bonding through feeding

To feed a person, baby or otherwise, establishes a bond, the significance of which is never lost between both parties. Watching someone eat and enjoy their food is part of human contact and is the basis of many food programmes on TV. Many chefs will admit they enjoy preparing food and watching other people eat more than eating the food themselves. Watching your own child feed is even more special and you will be assured of 'many happy returns'. While breastfeeding is without doubt the best way, it does tend to marginalise the dad. A father's time will come, however, and food from dad's plate always tastes better than the child's own. My father used to 'sneak' in the bone from the Sunday joint as if this was some major commando war-time success. Ask us to eat up the meat on our own plates, however, and everyone was just too full for even one more bite, cake being the only exception to the rule. We

> The most enjoyable part of having a child was knowing that there was part of you in the total control of someone else. A feeling that you had given yourself.
>
> Father of two

accepted that my dad had somehow 'stolen' the bone from the gaze of my mother. Forbidden fruit indeed. This same game would be played out between mother and father with secretive pleadings of 'you can have this but don't tell your father'. Children desperately want unity of parenthood yet are quite happy to be part of this conspiracy, totally underestimating the true extent and nature of parental collusion.

What is important about these intimacies is not just the ability to talk, feed or play, it is the effect each has on the bond which develops between a very young person and an older one. A steep learning curve is involved with little to go on except what has been traditionally performed by mothers. Innovation is the key. We have everything to gain from experimentation.

> I communicated by touch. I had to touch him all the time. His head, his face, his hands, his feet.
>
> Father of one

The great outdoors
Getting out and shopping

Fathers often complain of having nowhere to take
their new baby when shopping and they need a fresh
nappy. One father told me of his attack on this
bastion of female dominance. He took his child into a
mother-and-baby room in a well-known store. He had
to fight for the attention of a female shop assistant
who told him in the time-honoured confession that
'it was more than her job was worth' to allow him
into the room. 'Are there naked women in there?' he
asked. 'Maybe there are toilets only for women?'

> There was a time when I felt self-conscious because of old-world opinions that a man with kids was strange. But my pride in my kids removed these inhibitions.
>
> Divorced father

Having been reassured to the negative on both counts, he strode in. Women holding small babies in the room responded rather as though King Herod had gatecrashed a bonny baby competition. Still determined, he sat down and changed his child's nappy amid total silence. Brave as this father was, he never did it twice. It is worth contacting stores in advance to find out about their facilities. Some men are using the toilets intended for disabled people as they often contain changing mats for babies. Thankfully things are changing.

Advances in shopping

> I had no problem with shopping except for the usual curious grabbing and eating anything within reach. I did dislike the end-of-the-month mega shop. They and I got bored. I'm not good at debating the price of different brands of baked beans.
>
> Father of three

There was a time when a man would not push a pram in public let alone carry a baby in a backpack or sling. However, as society's expectations of men as fathers changes, it is becoming common not only to see men with prams and buggies but also to see them doing the shopping for the family, along with their young baby, in supermarkets. It can be easy to run away with the idea that supermarkets are all run by managers who just love children. If they do, they only demonstrated their affection after the effects of competition began to bite into their profits. Thus the sudden change of heart. Most chains now emphasise the fact that their stores are family-friendly. With all the changes that are taking place, and to make your shopping life as easy as possible, it makes sense to phone around first. The message will not be lost on the managers as the number of calls increases.

Changes on the way

Parking

One of the nightmares for a parent is the availability of car parking spaces. Shopping means negotiating an obstacle course of speeding cars driven by frustrated drivers intent on leaving the area as soon as humanly possible; trolley parks that require a mint condition pound coin and are the furthest distance away from the last remaining car park space; bollards that are designed to prevent trolleys wandering but would double admirably as tank traps; and spaces so narrow that parking a car full of children means at least a respray after they open the doors. Parking dedicated to parents with children, close to the entrance, such as exists for disabled drivers, makes sense and is beginning to appear.

> I was not too happy pushing the pram, but I got to enjoy it, honest.
>
> Father of one

Access

While it may make sense to pack every square millimetre with sellable goods, a narrow aisle is asking for a mail train effect. Anyone who has watched a train pick up a mailbag while on the move will recognise the analogy when taking a trolley loaded with children down a supermarket aisle. It is at this point that the analogy ends. While the mailbag invariably arrives safely on board the speeding train, the extra large bottle of tomato ketchup ends its life as a spectacular pool on the floor.

Trolleys

Supermarkets appear to believe that families consist of one child. Furthermore, the trolley is designed for a baby who can sit, unaided, in a metal framework which is aerodynamically sound for folding away but has little to do with safety. A range of trolleys makes better sense and is being introduced into the larger stores.

Corridor of hell: the checkout

Waiting with children at a checkout bedecked with sweets is not just a dentist's nightmare. If ever there was a more nasty side to sale promotion in a supermarket, I cannot think of it.

Paradoxically, it is the single biggest reason for a parent not to go back to the same store again. Such cynical exploitation of children for profit, when the goods themselves cause harm and when the manner in which they are displayed is detrimental to parental control, puts pressure on parents and children and is tawdry, to say the least. When the same people who grasp for such profit deplore the breakdown in family values, it gives some insight into their perception of society. Thankfully there is a shift against such pressure-selling using children, but not before time. Look out for stores which have extra staff at checkouts to help with the packing. They have been trained to 'home in' on the customers with a crying or difficult child.

> When my three-year-old began to demolish the sweet display at the checkout, I turned to a woman behind me and said in a loud voice, 'Madam, kindly control your child' and walked on through the checkout. It was only spoiled by my son shouting 'Daddy' at full volume, clutching several bars of chocolate.
>
> Father of two, still

Changing rooms and toilets

Given the shift towards buying in bulk for a family, the time spent in a supermarket can be considerable. Children have small bladders, babies need to be changed. For men this presents two problems: finding a toilet and finding a toilet which caters for men to look after their children. While there has been recent improvement, some supermarkets have changing rooms only for mothers with the helpful provision that 'staff will find room for fathers'. Talk about feeling like a second-class citizen.

Eating

Just as children's bladders are small so are their stomachs. At some point children will balance their growing hunger against the illegality of ripping the nearest packet of biscuits open. Given the strength of the instinct for human survival, it takes little imagination to picture the scene of chaos. Having facilities for eating is not the same as facilitating for children. Most fast-food outlets have a limited menu for children and welcome them. Some will lay on special treats for birthdays. Restaurants are not usually so keen but will still have a special children's menu. I have found that politely asking for a smaller-sized adult meal or one between three, is usually supplied with good grace.

Crèche facilities

Obviously the answer to shopping with children is the same as working with children – get someone else to look after them. You can only play on the sympathy of the next-door neighbour or relative for so long. Some supermarkets have introduced crèche facilities which allows you, for a small fee, to get on with the job. Play areas are not quite the same thing but some of them are supervised. With the increased fear of abduction, it makes good sense to insist upon supervised care. Be sure to investigate the credentials of the supervisor.

Go with the flow

Many public places present particular difficulties for fathers. For example, how is a father supposed to change his daughter at the swimming pool? I once took my four-year-old daughter into a men's changing room and there was a flurry of bare male bums going to earth. Strangely, not one single man complained but there was also not one single piece of bare flesh to be seen. This is in complete contrast to bringing in my son. There is little alternative other than to ask a passing woman to take your daughter into the changing room for you. Women have no problem bringing their young sons into a female changing room. There may be good reason for not bringing a young girl into a room full of men getting changed, but I suspect it has more to do with society's expectations rather than with any danger to her physical well-being or mental stability. It helps to contact the pool before arriving; they can often arrange facilities.

Toilets present a similar problem. I sent my daughter into a female public toilet during a day at the zoo. After what seemed like an eternity, I could stand the agony and fear no longer, as thoughts of kidnapping and child slaves refused to leave my fevered brain, and I poked my head into the toilet shouting, 'I'm just a daddy, I'm just a daddy.' The woman who stood in front of the mirror gave me a look which combined 'if I only had a penny for every time I've heard that one' with a pity for men who get their kicks from hanging around women's loos. Finding a second door on the other side of the toilet through which my daughter had passed much earlier, and was now happily feeding the ducks, did not help deal with her sanguine expression of surprise at my hair-pulling consternation. With logic common only to young girls, she informed me quite sternly that, 'The ducks just had to be fed, Daddy.'

On the plus side

Like most imbalances, the predicted or expected role of the mother can have certain advantages when they are reversed. Sitting on an aeroplane, I had a father sitting behind with his three young children. It was not long before two men had been recruited into service as entertainers. They were serious businessmen with pinstriped suits and laptops. For the hour-long flight they became surrogate fathers. Dad sat with the youngest on his knee drinking his free drinks, thoughtfully provided by a female member of the cabin staff who cooed approvingly at the male attempts at role-reversal with comments such as, 'I am most impressed'. I could not tell her that this was as much a sexist comment as that of a male television sports commentator for a women's bowls competition, who remarked, 'There, she bowled as good as any man.'

Show a bit of leg

Sitting with four young children in a restaurant, in a holiday setting, when there should be a mum on hand, can raise the interest of both women and men. In such a situation, I was soon the centre of attention. From the looks of the women, children in arms, it was obvious that they were trying to work out my status. Had my wife died during the birth of our last child, her last wish that I find someone to be their new mum? Was I part of the increasing number of dads, their marriage asunder, given custody of the children because of some terrible indiscretion of my wife with a Hungarian tightrope walker? I lived the part with wan looks of helplessness, until en masse the women could stand it no longer and descended upon our table with offers of help. I felt pretty good until one of the women whispered in my ear, 'Marvellous, I do the same thing when I need a flat tyre changed.' Such was my lesson of true male emancipation. If you can't stand the heat, get out of the restaurant.

Safety

Such is the pressure upon our society, with the increase in road traffic, congested footpaths, and problems with public transport that carrying a baby can have its own problems. This is compounded by having more than one child to look after. Good quality, safe equipment is as essential as the knowledge of how to use it.

Slings and backpacks

A sling is a soft pouch which you strap onto yourself so that you can hold your baby in front of you. Some slings hold the baby on your back. The front-loaders can be useful as you can hold a conversation with your baby while walking. Shopping is also easier as you can watch out for the odd bags of flour which can be grabbed unnoticed when your baby is at the back rather than the front, although the sling is generally for much younger babies. However, many men find the sling uncomfortable and complain of painful backs. This is interesting as the sling is supposed to be the best way to carry a load and protect the back. I suspect, however, that all the tests were carried out on women who just might have a different load-bearing design to men given that women may carry the unborn child in a not too dissimilar position.

A backpack is like a rucksack with a frame, which you can use to carry your baby on your back. It is only suitable for babies who can support their back and neck. Most come with strapping to adjust the way a child is carried. If they are held too high in the frame they can fall out when you bend over. Most of the accidents which occur with the use of backpacks and slings happen when the person carrying them falls. They are not designed for use on a bicycle and are particularly dangerous when used on a bike with dropped handlebars. Sharp braking can dislodge the child very easily and they are then exposed not only to the danger of the fall at speed but also to other traffic on the road.

Comfort, along with safety, is important. If you cannot tolerate the weight it will very soon discourage you from trying again. Try the sling or backpack on. Make sure it fits firmly and comfortably. Most of them have adjustable straps for the shoulders or neck. If the baby is held too low it will hurt your back. Too high, and you both become unstable.

Choose a backpack or sling which has buckles that clip together firmly rather than threaded straps which could slide loose. Make sure your baby cannot slide out through gaps in the sides, or fall out if the straps become loose. Some of the early designs had large gaps at the bottom through which a small baby could slip if not correctly supported by straps. Walking with a backpack or sling can make a baby's head swing about. Look for an adequate head support for babies who are less than three months old. Pace yourself. Even a small baby is a real addition to your weight when trying to walk any distance. The straps may cause welts on your shoulders. Wide, snugly fitting shoulder straps make life a great deal easier and safer. Having to constantly lift the backpack off sore shoulders may eventually dislodge your baby in an upwards direction.

Check backpacks for finger traps; small children can get their little fingers into gaps in the strapping which will constrict under strain. A constant crying can be interpreted as tiredness in a child who has, in fact, trapped their fingers in the backpack straps.

There is no reason why you should not buy second-hand equipment so long as it is in good order. A BSI kite mark is no guarantee of safety in second-hand equipment but it does give some indication of quality. Make sure the buckles and straps are in good condition and will still provide a safe adjustment for holding the baby securely. Watch out for perished material particularly where it covers the frame. Distorted frames are a good indication of excessive or inappropriate use. Using the empty backpack as an improvised rucksack is always a temptation.

Taking the baby out of a sling is relatively easy and safe. A backpack is a different matter. The safest way is to have a second person lift the baby out of the pack while you stand well-balanced or while you are sitting. It is tempting to balance the pack on its lower support and then lift out the child. Taking off a pack plus child on your own is not easy and can be dangerous. If no one is nearby to help, it should be done while kneeling on soft ground or carpeting.

Safe use:

- Adjust the straps properly for a comfortable, firm fit. A slack fit could let your baby slip out sideways or down.
- Wear sensible shoes for walking.
- Wrap your baby well in cold weather. Use the sling under a coat, or use a cape over a backpack.
- Do not carry your baby in a sling while you're cooking.
- A backpack can make your baby taller than you are. Watch out for doorways and low signs. Similarly, branches of trees and bushes can whip back as you pass and catch your baby in the face.

I didn't even notice that the backpack had become very light until one of the kids commented that my son was no longer in it. As we trudged up the forest path he had grabbed an overhanging branch. We found him a few yards back down the trail, quite happy playing in the leaf mould. I shudder every time I think about it.

Father of five

Transport

There is a wide range of transport available for babies. You may choose to have more than one item to use at different ages, or to buy one adaptable item to last from baby to toddler. All of them have some form of restraint harness or straps which should always be used no matter how short the journey. Most serious accidents involving prams and pushchairs happen through falls caused by not having the child securely restrained.

Carrycots

Look for a carrycot that is at least 19 centimetres (7 1/2 inches) deep. Shallow-sided cots are cheaper and easier to use but can be very dangerous. The safety of the cot when being carried depends upon the handles. Make sure it has strong handles which are wide enough to be carried in comfort and which meet over the cot so as not to force your hands apart when carrying. Second-hand carrycots are often perfectly suitable, particularly as they often see only limited use. Make sure the handles are in good condition and are firmly attached.

When travelling in a car, your baby is safer in a specially designed rear-facing baby car seat. These are often expensive but give a considerable amount of protection compared to the carrycot lying on the floor of the car.

Pushchairs and buggies

There is an enormous range of pushchairs and buggies to choose from. Some have moveable seats which can be fully reclined to take a very young baby. With others, you can take off the seat and use the chassis with a carrycot. Some fold flat, others fold up even smaller into an umbrella shape. There has to be some sacrifice in stability and safety when a complicated folding mechanism is employed. Careful use will minimise the risk of harm from a buggy or pushchair with such mechanisms.

Injuries to babies and children are common with these forms of transport. This is probably a reflection of their popularity and common use but it also indicates that even with the safest machines mistakes are being made which, in the main, cannot be prevented by changes in design.

Safe use:

- Get into the habit of always using a harness in a pram, pushchair or buggy, even when your baby is very young.

- Do not let children climb about on a pram, pushchair or buggy. They may fall off or tip it over.

- Don't overload a pram, pushchair or buggy with children or shopping. It may overbalance. Most buggies face forward so a fall from overloading the handles causes the baby to hit their head as they fall backwards. The force of the impact is enhanced by the weight of the shopping which may add to any injury from broken glass or caustic chemicals.

- Make sure all the safety locks are fully in place every time you use a pushchair or buggy. This will stop it folding up suddenly with your child inside.

- Only put your child into the pushchair or buggy once it has been set up and adjusted. It is very easy to trap fingers when it is being set up or folded.

Check your pram, pushchair or buggy every two or three months. Make sure that the brakes still hold on a slope, that the wheels are solid and that the safety catches work well. If you find a problem, check with the shop where you bought it.

Safety in cars

The law dictates proper restraint for children in cars. Following the basic rules for car safety can dramatically cut the risk of serious injury in a crash.

Choice of restraint

Although looks and design may be important, the choice of the particular type of restraint really depends on the weight of the child. From birth to about nine months old there's a choice between the rear-facing baby carriers and the traditional carrycot restraints. Baby carriers are safer than carrycot restraints, take up only one seat in the car and can be used either in the front or back seat (wherever there is an adult seat belt). Baby carriers are also easier to lift in and out of the car and can be used indoors. Carrycot restraints can only be used on the back seat.

For children weighing between 10 and 18 kilograms you need one of the child car seats which sit on the back seat. Four-point anchorage models are safer than those using only two. Alternatively, child seats secured by adult seat belts are available. Older, bigger children up to eleven years old need booster seats to make adult seat belts work effectively. Alternatively the back seat can be fitted with child harnesses to be used with or without booster seats. These padded seats lift the child up into

> After I saw what had happened, I went out and bought a set of child seat belts for my daughter's children. I still have nightmares over the accident.
>
> Consultant, accident and emergency department of a busy Belfast hospital. She treated a number of children, all of whom died after being thrown through the front windscreen of a car driven by their mother. The mother survived.

the harness which then fits securely across their body. They must be used correctly and need to be restrained themselves and not left loose on top of the seat. Children generally favour these seats as they allow for better vision while travelling. Once over eleven years old children can use an adult seat belt without a booster seat.

Harnesses and reins

Every year about five hundred children are killed in the UK while walking or playing in the street. Another twenty-four thousand are injured. Most of these children are unsupervised or have no restraints. A child will run out onto a road even if being held by the hand, giving the father little chance to retrieve them and giving even less time for the driver of an approaching car to avoid them. Harnasses and reins can be used for restraining children while walking, or in a seat, pram, buggy, carrycot, high chair or supermarket trolley. Forget to harness your child in, and he could topple or get tipped out. Choose a harnass that is easy to adjust, has strong straps, and is easy to fasten on a wriggling toddler. Some parents have found that harnesses with clips on the harness itself, rather than on the carrier, are easier to cope with.

> I was just walking with him when he darted out into the road. The driver didn't have a chance.
>
> Father of five-year-old, killed by a car. I sat with him in the accident and emergency department while he waited for his wife who was working at the time of the accident.

Complacency

It may appear pedantic, even bureaucratic, to outline the safety aspect of carrying babies and children but, as fathers take more and more responsibility for carrying their children, in the car or otherwise, it is important that dangers are understood and prevented.

So who looks after the children?

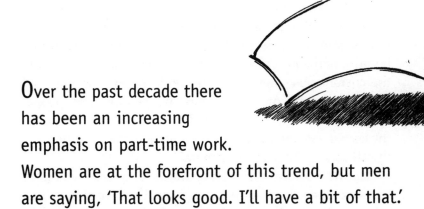

Over the past decade there
has been an increasing
emphasis on part-time work.
Women are at the forefront of this trend, but men
are saying, 'That looks good. I'll have a bit of that.'
With the shift in employment patterns, it is
becoming clearer that there will be a big changes
in the way we look after our children.

Changing roles

The changing roles of the sexes has shown that paradoxically there are some areas where men are disadvantaged. A great deal of this comes from the way money comes into the family home. How are men, for instance, going to cope with changes, such as women being breadwinners? Paradoxically, society has not given opportunities for men to be fathers. We are still in the position of women looking after children, men going out to work and when this breaks down there is little to support men in their role as carers of children. We need to impress upon government that as fathers we should have the right to share in the upbringing of our children rather than simply being seen as providers.

> When my wife went part-time at her job I felt annoyed. She spent time at home and looked after the kids. With all the redundancies at our plant I applied for part-time work rather than lose my job completely. It was the best thing I ever did. Now I actually get to see the kids before they go to bed.
>
> Father of three

Sacrifice

There is still a resistance towards discussion of these issues at work. Many men have to sacrifice their family life in order to be able to pursue careers. The sacrifice, however, works both ways, and families can be effectively fatherless because of the pressure of work. This has been amplified by the current obsession with efficiency where one man will often do the job once performed by two or more people. Very little attention has been directed towards the effects these changes have upon individual men, their families and the structure of society in general.

Clear decisions are needed about the emphasis we put on work compared to family and play. The overtime which will provide for the CD player, and the promotion which brings with it extra responsibility and more time away from home, will all have to be considered in the light of being a committed father, rather than simply fathering children. A father's presence is particularly important during the early developing years of our children.

> Money ruled our family. I couldn't take time off because I had to pay for the freezer, the television and the car. When my partner got a job I felt threatened at first. I was the one who paid for everything. It took a bit of getting used to, like.
>
> Father of two

Lack of back-up

When a reduction of staff forces an individual to take sole

responsibility for a particular area at work, there is immense pressure not to take time way from work for any reason. The pressure can be so intense that men will take work home with them, further compounding their already reduced contact with their children. Unless work practices include an element of redundancy, this pressure will affect both the individual's family life and their personal capacity to function. Many employers now recognise the value of allowing employees to get on with their work as free as possible from stress generated from whatever direction, particularly the home environment.

> When I asked my boss could I have a few weeks off because my son was coming out of hospital, he asked if I was still married. I wanted to be there, as well as my wife, but jobs are hard to find.
>
> Father of child with leukaemia

Divorce and single parents

These changes in the workplace take place alongside a significant shift in attitudes towards marriage and long-term relationships. With divorce and separation rates on the increase, children are often involved in family break-ups. While it has been shown that children are better off once their parents have split up if there is violence or extreme levels of stress involved, it would obviously be better if the family unit did not need to divide in the first place. The trick is to keep families together from desire rather than coercion.

> There was a wall between us. I could almost feel it. We used to use the children to hurt each other, like swords. That was the worst bit. Now I don't even ask about my former wife's partner when the kids come round. I wish I had them instead of her, though.
>
> Divorced father, paying maintenance

There are a large number of voluntary bodies which offer advice and support when separation occurs. Sometimes these only produce temporary relief and may even prolong the agony. Often, however, relationship counselling through organisations such as Relate can prove very valuable (see Contacts and Resources). Even in cases where it fails, those couples who do separate, do so less acrimoniously. Increasingly, however, there is a demand for permanent answers to what is becoming a major problem.

Parenting skills at school

How do we supply life skills to our children, including parenting skills, to prepare them for dealing as adults with their own children? It is remarkable that while we control children's education through the national curriculum, there is little effort made to prepare them for their greatest challenge, that of being a parent themselves. It will take a positive attitude from the government and educational bodies to help children understand the changing role of fathers and the need for flexibility in the way we employ both men and women to allow them contact with their children.

Changes within the home over the past decade

Not only have there been dramatic changes in employment patterns which have had their effect upon the family, there have also been changes taking place within the family home itself.

Life expectancy

Both men and women are, on average, living longer. Traditionally older relatives were looked after within the family home and this provided contact between the older and younger generations. With the expense of nursing homes, older relatives who need constant care are now being looked after in the home of immediate relatives. The onset of this care can be as sudden as a phone call informing the family that their previously mobile but elderly aunt has fallen and sustained a fractured hip.

Women were always seen as the obvious carers but this is changing and men are finding themselves as both fathers and carers within the home. Little provision is made within the workplace for women and less for men to be able to perform these caring responsibilities. This places greater strain upon fathers and their relationship with their children. Surprisingly, 53 per cent of men compared with 54 per cent of women currently act as carers. This figure is inevitably going to increase.

Women returning to work after childbirth

Not only are more women taking up employment, but they are also increasingly returning to work after they have had a child. Where there is little difference in pay between the father and mother, the decision on who should remain at home to look after the children is no longer automatic. Society still has a jaundiced view of the man remaining at home while the woman goes out to work, but this is changing under the pressure of events.

Family-friendly policies

Some employers have taken the lead and are introducing employment practices which allow parents to have increased contact with their families. This is not simply altruism. Increasingly employers are recognising the value of policies which are family-friendly. Not only do these policies help to retain highly experienced staff but they also reduce absenteeeism and improve job satisfaction and therefore the

The first we knew of her accident was when social services rang us to tell us we had to pick her up from the hospital. I hadn't seen her for twenty-six years, and suddenly she lived with us. Two of the children had to move into our bedroom. I didn't really mind, but we had different ideas on how we were going to live in the future. That's all changed now.

Father of four who looks after his 82-year-old aunt with a fractured hip

quality of work produced by both men and women. The HSBC Bank, for instance, has established nurseries to allow both fathers and mothers to return to work. They have extended this to holiday play schemes and have maternity leave longer than the legal minimum period required.

It is gradually dawning on employers that for every £1 they invest in family-friendly policies they derive £3 in improved work from both men and women.

Part of the reason why we split up was over money. I felt that I was just a cash dispenser, a hole in the wall. I wanted to get closer to my kids but I had to work to get money to keep them safe. Now I still supply the money and see even less of them than I did before.

Divorced father of five

I used to work fifty-six hours and bring home the accounts. The kids were in bed when I got home and were still there when I went out in the morning. I may as well have been on my own. Now I share my job with a woman who also works part-time. I write, play the guitar, play with the kids. We sold the second car and the caravan. The kids have less money and more dad. Tough, I tell them, as I fight them all on the bed.

Father of four

A career break seemed like a passport to extinction. It certainly was a break – I found my children for the first time. I will keep working as an architect, but not in my children's time.

Father of three who went from house architect to mushroom farmer to landscape architect

First aid

Most accidental
injuries are minor
and can be treated
using simple first aid
measures. But in the
unlikely event of a serious
accident or sudden illness,
knowledge of first aid techniques could
help you to save a child's life. By following the basic
guidelines provided here you will be able to deal with
most day-to-day accidents and injuries. Information
on dealing with emergencies is also provided.

EMERGENCIES

There are three key things to remember in any emergency situation:

- remain calm and confident
- do all you can to help but do not put yourself in danger
- do not give the child anything to eat or drink

Seek urgent medical attention for:

- head injury with bleeding from eyes, ears or nose, drowsiness or vomiting
- loss of consciousness
- broken bone or dislocation
- severe chest pain or breathlessness
- sudden severe abdominal pain that will not go away
- unresolved choking and difficult breathing
- severe bleeding

Sometimes, the quickest way of getting medical help is to take the child directly to the accident and emergency department of your local hospital. But call an ambulance and do not move the child if:

- you think he or she may have a back or neck injury, or any other injury that could be made worse by movement
- the person is in shock, unconscious or has stopped breathing, and needs your constant attention

Shock

Anyone who has experienced an injury may go into shock. They may become pale, sweaty, drowsy and confused. A child in shock needs urgent medical attention. While waiting for help, remain calm and reassure the child, but do not give them anything to eat or drink. If they are unconscious, lay the child on their back with their legs raised, loosen any tight clothing and keep them warm.

Emergency first aid

The recovery position

This is a safe position for an unconscious child, which allows easy breathing and prevents choking if the child vomits. After checking the child is breathing normally, turn them on their side. Ensure that the airway is clear by pulling the jaw forward and tipping the head back slightly.

Mouth-to-mouth resuscitation

A child may stop breathing for many different reasons, including drowning, electric shock or poisoning. A few simple stops can save their life:

1 Lay the child on a firm surface. Tilt the head back and lift the chin to open the air passages.

2 Check to see if they are breathing for ten seconds. If they are, place them in the recovery position described above.

3 If they are still not breathing, pinch the nose shut. Take a deep breath and place your mouth firmly over the child's mouth. Breathe into the mouth twice – the chest should rise.

4 Continue to give a breath every six seconds. In children under three breathe gently once every three seconds.

5 Do not stop until the child breathes alone or medical help arrives.

Cardiopulmonary resuscitation (CPR)

CPR is a life-saving technique for someone whose heart (pulse) has stopped. It is best used only if you have been trained in the technique. The instructions below are to refresh your memory.

1 Check for circulation by feeling for a pulse at the carotid artery in the neck, and generally looking for signs of recovery. If there is no breathing or pulse start CPR.

2 Place the child in the same position as for mouth-to-mouth resuscitation.

3   Kneel beside the child and place the heel of one of your palms on the lower half of the breastbone, with the heel of the other palm on top.

4   With straight arms, lean forward so that your shoulders are over the child's breastbone, and press the breastbone down, using two-finger pressure only.

5   Allow the breastbone to return to the original position.

6   Repeat the procedure, pressing at the rate of one hundred compressions a minute.

7   Give mouth-to-mouth at the rate of two breaths into the mouth for every fifteen chest compressions.

8   Do not stop until the pulse returns or medical help arrives.

Telephone 999 for an ambulance.

Basic first aid

Bites and stings

Insect bites and stings can be painful but they are not usually serious, even in children. Most can be treated with simple, common sense remedies without needing the attention of your doctor.

Apply a cold compress to insect bites and stings. Remove bee stings with tweezers by gripping the base of the sting nearest to the skin to avoid squeezing the poison sac. Remove ticks by covering them with a smear of petroleum jelly (for example, Vaseline), which blocks their breathing holes and causes them to drop off. Simply pulling at the tick or trying to burn it off can leave the head in the skin, leading to infection.

Seek medical attention if:

• the child has a known allergy to bites and stings

• the sting cannot be removed

• there is infection around the site

• the child experiences fever or shortness of breath

Animal bites need urgent medical attention, as they may become infected if not treated. Small animal bites should be thoroughly cleaned with soap and water and covered with a sterile dressing. For serious bites, apply direct pressure with a clean cloth to control the bleeding.

Broken bones and dislocations

Broken bones and dislocations always need immediate medical attention. They can be very painful, and you can help by reassuring the child and keeping them still.

Broken limbs

Steady and support the limb with your hands. If a leg is broken, place padding around it to prevent movement. A broken arm or collarbone should be supported on the affected side of the body. Seek medical attention at the accident and emergency unit of your local hospital.

Injured neck or spine

Keep the injured child as still as possible. It is essential not to move someone with a neck or spine injury unless they are in imminent danger of further injury. If the casualty becomes unconscious, carefully place them in the recovery position while keeping the spine in line at all times. Call an ambulance immediately.

Dislocated joints

Never try to force a joint back into place. Simply support the limb and seek emergency help.

Burns and scalds

Any burn or scald requires immediate action. For minor injuries, carefully remove watches, jewellery, shoes and anything else that may cause constriction if swelling occurs. Cool the affected area with cold water for at least ten minutes, then cover with a light, non-fluffy material. For a limb, kitchen film or a polythene bag may be used. Do not burst any blisters and do not apply any cream or ointments. The exception is mild sunburn which may be soothed with a lotion like calamine. Seek medical attention if:

- the burn is larger than the size of your hand
- the burn is on the face
- the skin is broken

Severe burns need urgent medical attention. Cool the burn down, cover it with a sterile dressing, and get the child to your local accident and emergency department immediately or call for an ambulance. While waiting for the ambulance, lay the child down and raise their legs. This helps keep blood available for the vital organs. Do not remove clothes if they are sticking to the skin.

Choking

Choking happens surprisingly often. Immediate action is vital, so it is important to know the correct steps to follow:

- Check inside the mouth and remove any obstruction.
- If you can't see or feel any obstruction, bend the child over and use the flat of your hand to slap them firmly between the shoulder blades five times to dislodge the blockage; use a more gentle tap for small children.
- If choking continues, try the abdominal thrust: stand behind the child, put both arms around their waist and interlock your hands. Then pull sharply upwards below the ribs, telling them to cough as you do so. Be careful when performing this procedure on children – their bones are much more delicate than an adult's – and do not perform on children under three.
- Repeat this procedure until the blockage is removed.

If the blockage is not completely cleared, or the person continues to have trouble breathing, seek urgent medical attention.

Cuts, grazes and bleeding

For a minor cut, press the wound with a clean fabric pad for a few minutes to help stop the bleeding. For a cut on an arm or leg, elevate the limb. Water may be used to wipe around the edge of the cut or graze. Once clean, apply a dressing, e.g. a plaster.

Seek medical attention if:

- the cut is deep and the edges cannot be pulled together
- severe redness or swelling develops after a couple of days (this may be a sign of an infection)

Severe bleeding from a wound needs immediate medical attention. While waiting for expert help, lay the child down and raise the injured part of the body above the level of the heart to help reduce blood loss. Place a clean cloth against the wound and press firmly. Secure this pad in place.

Never attempt to control the bleeding by using a tourniquet to constrict the artery of an arm or a leg.

Nosebleeds

Nosebleeds are common and most are easily dealt with. Sit the child down, leaning slightly forward, and tell them to breathe through the mouth. Then pinch the nose firmly for about ten minutes. Seek medical help if the bleeding continues for more than thirty minutes or if you suspect the nose is broken.

Head injuries

Bangs on the head are common, particularly amongst children. Few need the attention of your doctor, but occasionally a head injury can cause bleeding inside the skull, which needs urgent medical treatment. This bleeding can take place soon after the injury, or up to six months later.

For a minor knock or bump to the head, sit the child down as they may be dizzy, and place a cold, damp cloth on the affected area. You may want to provide a basin in case the child vomits.

Seek urgent medical attention if:

- the child experiences double vision or hearing loss
- repeated vomiting, fits or convulsions occur

- the child seems confused
- discharge appears from the nose, eyes or ears
- the pain continues after three days

Remember that these symptoms may appear some time after the initial incident. If they do, visit your doctor.

Poisoning

Accidental poisoning is one of the most common reasons for children to need emergency treatment. Seek expert medical advice immediately. You can provide important help for the doctors by trying to find out what has caused the poisoning, how much was taken and when, and by taking any containers and remains of tablets, liquids, plants or samples of vomit to the hospital with you.

- If the child becomes unconscious, place them in the recovery position and if breathing stops, begin mouth-to-mouth resuscitation following the procedure described at the beginning of this section.

Sprains, strains and bruising

Sprains and strains often occur during everyday tasks in the house or garden, or while playing sport. To remind yourself how to deal with a sprain, strain or bruising, remember RICE (rest, ice, compress, elevation).

- Rest the injured part as much as possible.
- Immediately after the injury, pack the area with ice wrapped in a cloth – a bag of frozen peas works well – to reduce swelling. Keep the ice in place for about twenty minutes.
- Gently compress the injury and bind the area with an elastic bandage so it is well supported, but make sure it doesn't restrict blood flow.
- To minimise swelling, keep the injured part elevated as much of the time as possible.

Be patient with sprains and strains: they don't heal overnight. When the pain subsides, exercise the limb or joint gently to prevent stiffness. Only resume normal activities when there is no pain or swelling. Bruising also takes several days to get better. It will start off blue, purple or black, fading to yellow before it disappears.

Seek medical attention if:

- you think there may be a broken bone – immobilise the area with padding and seek aid immediately

- symptoms don't improve

- bruising remains after several days

Useful contacts

The British Red Cross
Tel: 020 7235 5454
information@redcross.org.uk

St John Ambulance
Tel: 0171 235 5231
www.st-john-ambulance.org.uk

Both organisations provide information and courses in first aid.

A–Z

The ultimate survival package for
children's problems and illnesses

Abdominal pain

Have they just eaten a large amount of fruit or foods they do not usually eat? **YES** Overeating, especially of acid fruit, can cause tummy pain. Try simple indigestion remedies like milk. If the symptoms do not improve or if they worsen within forty-eight hours, call your doctor.

Are they constipated? **YES** Not enough fluids, particularly in hot weather can cause constipation in children. If the symptoms do not improve or if they develop a new symptom such as vomiting call your doctor. Otherwise ask your pharmacist for advice.

Is it painful for them to pass water or they are passing water much more often than usual? **YES** They may have a urinary infection. Call your doctor.

Is there a fever (their temperature is over 38°C/100.4°F) and vomiting, meaning that they are unable to keep down any fluids? **YES** **See 'Fever in Children'** Children rapidly dehydrate when there is a fever and they cannot take fluids due to vomiting. Call your doctor.

Is there any blood in their vomit or bowel motions? **YES** **See 'Diarrhoea in Children'/'Vomiting in Children'** Blood in either vomit or motions needs medical attention.

Is the child screaming constantly, and/or vomiting and movement of any kind makes it worse? **YES** A blockage of the bowel is a possibility. Call your doctor.

Home treatment

- Reassure the child and try to encourage rest.
- If they are not vomiting try giving paracetamol (follow the instructions on the packet to ensure the correct dose for the child's age).
- Give only small amounts of clear fluids for twelve hours, then small amounts of their usual food (without milk) until the child feels better.
- If the condition gets worse or new symptoms develop, call your doctor.

Allergies

There is a difference between something irritating the skin or digestive system and an allergic reaction by the body to a particular substance or food. When stimulated by an allergen – the cause of the allergy – the body's reaction can range from a mild flush to a serious and life-threatening condition. Thankfully this is rare and many people will suffer for years without realising they are the victim of their own body's defence system. Allergies in children can be dangerous. Asthma attacks can be triggered by droppings from house mites. Products containing peanuts can actually kill susceptible people. Allergic conditions include:

- Coeliac disease: gluten is particularly nasty on the lining of the intestine. You can buy gluten-free bread.
- Hay fever and allergic asthma: pollen, house mites, pets and mouldy dust can all cause respiratory and nasal problems.
- Eczema: contact dermatitis is well recognised. Cement dust is particularly bad for the condition.
- Urticaria (itchy hives): thankfully these tend to be harmless even if they are very annoying. Nettles will produce it in susceptible children but so will foods like strawberries or seafood.

Most allergies are recognised by their effects on the skin.

Symptoms

Immediate reactions can affect the whole body or just around the contact area. For some children the skin can become sore and broken with even the slightest exposure to the allergen. Symptoms include:

- itchiness
- a blotchy red rash over the body
- blocked or running nose
- eye irritation
- fluid retention

More serious reactions can lead to:

- chest tightness
- shortness of breath
- fatigue

Causes

There are a wide range of possible allergens and a great deal depends on your child's own particular allergy state. They are more likely to suffer from strong allergic reactions if they have hay fever, asthma or have had a reaction to a particular substance in the past. Subsequent contact, for instance the second time they are stung by a bee, can be worse than the first time.

Possible allergens include:

- foods such as peanuts, seafood and strawberries
- dairy and grain produce for a longer-term allergy
- soap powders
- latex, e.g. rubber gloves, plasters
- nickel jewellery or watches
- hair dye
- cement dust
- eggs

Prevention

Once the allergy is established, its cause must be either removed or avoided. Substitutes for particular foods or materials are often available and do not provoke an allergic response.

- Use a filter in the vacuum cleaner to remove dust mite droppings.
- Check food labels for potentially allergic contents such as peanut products.

Complications

Serious allergic reactions can be fatal. Long-term reactions can cause debilitation even after there is no further contact with the allergenic substance. Anaphylactic shock is an extreme allergic reaction. Immediately after contact there is itchiness, swelling of the lips and throat, a drop in blood pressure and finally collapse. Ring 999 immediately if anaphylactic shock is suspected.

Self-help

- Wash off any of the suspected allergens if they are on the skin.
- Calamine lotion reduces the itchiness of the rash.
- Bathe in a cool bath with a large spoonful of baking soda.
- Use a hay fever spray for nasal problems.
- Antihistamine creams or sprays help with localised allergic reactions.
- Carry antihistamine tablets in case of an attack.
- If your child has ever had an anaphylactic shock attack, you should also carry injectable adrenaline from your doctor.

More help

You should make an appointment to see your doctor if:

- your home treatment fails to work
- you are considering a significant diet change for the child
- there are any serious allergic reactions (see above)
- there are any new and unexpected reactions

Advice and support can also be found through the Anaphylaxis Campaign, a national UK charity and self-help organsiation. Tel: 01252 542029.

Antibiotics

In cases where children will get better without antibiotics, it makes sense for your doctor not to prescribe them. Your body's defence system can often protect against infection without the need for antibiotics. Your doctor will be able to recognise whether your child has an infection that needs antibiotics, so you should not always expect to be given a prescription. Doctors need to prescribe antibiotics with care because inappropriate use of antibiotics can be dangerous for individual patients and for the whole population.

Overuse of antibiotics can also cause resistance and result in them not working in the future. This is a very worrying trend, especially for patients with serious life-threatening infections.

Harmful side-effects

Potential side effects are another reason why doctors are cautious about prescribing antibiotics. Some antibiotic treatment can cause side effects such as stomach upset and thrush. More serious, life-threatening side effects can also occur.

Antibiotic facts

- Antibiotics have no effect on viral infections, e.g. colds, flu and most sore throats. Viral infections are much more common than bacterial infections.

- Inappropriate use of antibiotics can encourage the development of resistant bacteria. This could mean that the antibiotic may not work when your child really needs it.

- Some antibiotics have harmful side effects such as diarrhoea and allergic reactions.

- Antibiotics do not just attack the infection they are prescribed for; they can also kill useful bacteria which normally protect you against other infections such as thrush.

- There are effective alternative remedies for managing the symptoms of many infections.

- If your child is prescribed antibiotics ensure they take the medication according to the instructions. Although they may begin to feel better, they must take the full course of antibiotics to prevent their illness coming back. Not taking the full course of antibiotics may lead to future antibiotic resistance.

Asthma

For reasons we are not sure of, asthma is on the increase. Part of the problem may be pollution in our environment, particularly from exhaust fumes. Thankfully the number of people who die from asthma attacks are declining but with around two thousand deaths each year, asthma should be taken very seriously. The problem can appear at any stage in life but is more common in children. Some people find the severity of the condition decreases as they get older. Modern treatments will prevent or stop the vast majority of asthma attacks.

Symptoms

The first sign of an attack can be as simple as a repeated cough which can rapidly develop into a frightening breathlessness and tightness in the chest. This is usually painless but after an attack there may be muscle strain which can ache. In the early stages a wheeze can be heard as the child breathes out. If they are suffering from a very serious attack there may be little or no wheeze or even the sound of breathing. They tend to sit up straight with their head slightly back and lips pursed. With severe attacks their lips may turn blue and they will be unable to speak. This is an emergency and you must dial 999.

Causes

Some forms of asthma are triggered, though not caused, by things such as pollen, hay or house dust. Other forms seem to just happen with no apparent reason although stress or a recent chest infection can act as triggers. Children who have hay fever or other allergies are most likely to develop asthma.

Prevention

There is as yet no way of preventing the condition but you can reduce the number and severity of attacks particularly for a child with the allergic type of asthma. Keep a record of when and where they were with each attack. You may find it ties in with certain activities at school, the presence of a particular pet, the pollen count on that day or even what they had to eat. Some of these things cannot be changed but simple things like covering mattresses with a plastic cover to prevent dust mites, or keeping certain flowers out of the house, may make a difference. House mites' faeces are powerful triggers for some asthma sufferers. Many vacuum cleaners can now be fitted with special filters which prevent them being blown into the air.

Complications

Badly controlled asthma can be dangerous especially when the early warning signs are ignored.

Self-help

General good health is important as is regular activity. If the child becomes breathless during activity tell him/her to try using their inhaler before they start the activity rather than during it. Check their peak flow regularly and compare with your record of attacks. It may point out triggers. Resist the temptation to skip preventative medicine just because the child feels fine at the time.

Nebulisers are often supplied by local surgeries on a loan basis or from support groups. These are very useful for children who find hand-held inhalers difficult to use and can stop an asthma attack in its tracks. In an emergency while away from such machines, cut the large round end off a plastic lemonade bottle and fire the inhaler into the open end while the child breathes through the narrow screw-top hole.

Staying calm is vital when dealing with a child suffering an asthma attack. Find their inhaler and help them to use it, reassure them, give them nothing to drink and allow them to sit in any position they find most comfortable; do not force them to lie down. If there is a nebuliser available use it sooner rather than later. Dial 999 if it is a serious attack.

Bed wetting
Enuresis

Bed wetting is very common yet can cause unnecessary concern to both parent and child.

- Around three out of four toddlers stay dry all night by age three to four.
- One in five still wet the bed by age five.
- One in ten children suffer bed wetting by age six.
- In a class of thirty school children aged seven to nine, two will have bed-wetting problems.
- Boys are more likely than girls to wet their beds.
- Bed wetting may start again during stressful times or during illness.

Symptoms

Most children are not aware of wetting the bed until they wake up. This can make them very frightened of being told off and lead to more bed wetting.

Causes

- It is poorly understood.
- There is a natural variation in the development of bladder control.
- It may be a symptom of illness, such as diabetes or a urinary tract infection, especially if in a child who was previously dry through the night.

Prevention

Parental reassurance and understanding are vital. It is not a sign of laziness. Children have little or no control over this condition.

- Making the child feel guilty will make things worse.
- Try to be understanding and supportive.
- Avoid fizzy drinks, tea and coffee just before bedtime as they stimulate the production of urine.

- Put a potty close to the bed and leave a night light on.

- Some psychologists recommend that you simply wait for the problem to pass.

Complications

Unsympathetic responses to your child will undermine their confidence and may well make the problem worse so that they may find themselves losing control of their bladder in stressful circumstances such as at school.

Self-help

- Make sure your child goes to the toilet before going to bed.

- Leave fresh bedclothes next to them so they can change the bed themselves.

- Keep a flannel-covered rubber sheet nearby so you can put it over the wet sheets.

- Set an alarm clock to ring two to three hours after your child falls asleep. Set the clock a little later each night.

- Try making a game of bladder-stretching or stream interruption exercises. Counting to ten before releasing the flow of urine helps them develop important muscles.

- Obtain a bed-wetting alarm. (This is best suited for children five years and older.) Modern enuresis alarms have moisture sensors that attach directly to the underwear. At the first drop of liquid, a buzzer sounds, waking up the child. These alarms are free on loan from your health visitor.

More help

ERIC (Enuresis Resource and Information Centre) supplies alarms and information packs for parents. Tel: 0117 960 3060.

If these tips do not work or if you think there may be an infection, talk to your doctor.

Blood in the white of the eye
Subconjunctival haemorrhage

Seeing bright red blood over the white of the eye can be quite alarming yet it is completely harmless and very common. It is often seen in babies. Tiny blood vessels beneath the protective layer (conjunctiva) burst and a small amount of blood becomes trapped under it.

Symptoms

The blood appears very quickly. Generally it will be over one part of the white of the eye but sometimes may cover most or all of it.

Causes

Minor injury or a blow to the eye may cause one of the tiny blood vessels beneath the conjunctiva to burst. Coughing, sneezing, straining at the toilet or even hard crying can also cause it. It is common in babies and children when they cry for long periods.

Complications

There is nothing to be done except cover the eye if it embarrasses you. The blood will turn purple black after a few days and look like a bruise. Within a week or so it should disappear altogether.

Action

Unless there was trauma involved there is no need for a medical examination as the blood will gradually disperse on its own.

Boils

Boils are generally caused by infected hair follicles. When the body fights the commonest cause of boils, the bacterium staphylococcus, it builds a protective wall around the infection, preventing it from spreading. Unfortunately this also impedes the body's natural defences from attacking the bacteria and a cyst or boil develops. After a certain length of time the skin lying over the boil will break down, releasing the pus. Carbuncles are just collections of boils very close together and are thankfully not seen very often these days.

Symptoms

It's hard to miss a boil. A painful red lump appears on the skin which gradually gets larger and more painful. The area around the boil is also very tender and slightly inflamed. After a few days a white or yellow 'head' forms which means the boil is about to burst through the skin to release the pus and ease the pain. Some boils will disappear without actually releasing the pus through the skin.

Causes

Being run down or suffering from an illness which lowers the body's defence against infection can increase the risk from boils. Dirty skin is not a cause of boils. Overwashing with antiseptic soaps may even increase the risk.

Prevention

There is no real prevention against boils but if they occur regularly children should see the doctor.

Complications

Some boils can persist and come back again in the same place. This may leave a scar.

Self-help

Once the head has formed you can encourage the boil to break by using warm water compresses. Soak some cotton wool in warm water mixed with a couple of spoonfuls of salt. Press it against the boil, gently squeezing at the same time. Do not use the highly dangerous method of putting the mouth of a heated bottle to the boil then cooling the bottle to draw the pus. It can release the infection into the blood stream and may leave a scar.

Some doctors will prescribe antibiotics but others feel that this may delay the natural eruption of the boil through the skin. Once the head is formed some doctors will lance the boil by cutting into the head and breaking down all the layers within the boil, allowing it to drain freely.

More help

Ask your doctor.

Chickenpox

Children exposed to the virus develop chickenpox seven to twenty-one days later. In most cases there is no evidence of the impending illness before the rash appears.

Symptoms

A mild fever, stomach ache and general malaise can occur a day or two before the flat, red rash appears. The rash generally begins on the scalp, face and back, but can spread to any body surface although it is rarely seen on the palms of the hands or soles of the feet.

- Intensely itchy, tiny clear blisters soon follow.

- Fresh red spots are usually seen next to blisters and crusts.

- Most children are free from chicken pox in less than two weeks.

Complications

Complications are very rare, although chickenpox can occasionally lead to encephalitis (inflammation of the brain), meningitis or pneumonia. Serious complications are more common in those children who are taking medicines such as steroids as they can lower the body's immune system. Ask your doctor for advice.

Prevention

This virus spreads quickly, especially between children. Sneezing, coughing, touching contaminated clothing and direct contact with the open blisters are all ways of catching this relatively harmless infection.

Self-help

There is no vaccination available at present.

- Use cool baths without soap every three to four hours for the first couple of days. Add a few tablespoons of sodium bicarbonate to the bath water.

- Calamine lotion gives temporary relief.

- Cotton socks on inquisitive hands will prevent too much scratching which can lead to infection.

- Antihistamines are available from your pharmacist. These help to reduce itching and promote sleep, so use them just before bedtime.

- Paracetamol helps reduce the fever. Do not give aspirin to children under twelve years of age.

- Ice lollies help to lower temperature, provide sugar and water and at the same time reduce the irritation of mouth infection. They may be given to children over four years of age.

More help

Call your doctor.

Childhood obesity

Obesity in children is increasing rapidly. Not only is obesity a health hazard while they are young, it sets a pattern for later life. Being overweight is linked to conditions such as diabetes and heart disease. Being overweight can also make the child the butt of other children's jokes and prevent them from taking part in sports activities. All this tends to affect their confidence and makes them more solitary by nature.

Weight gain can creep up as slowly on children as it does on adults. It can also happen very quickly if their level of activity drops suddenly, say by moving house with less area for playing.

Causes

There is a mix of causes and each will contribute to obesity.

Lack of exercise:

- Cycling or even walking to school is not as safe as it was. Parents are now more likely to take their children to school by car.

Sedentary playing:

- Television and computer games compete with games which involve physical activity.

Inappropriate diet:

- Children eat more sweets, partly because of advertising but also because society is more affluent.

- Fast food is overtaking traditionally prepared meals. Many involve coating food with fatty creams or batters.

- Poor fresh fruit consumption. Despite being more readily available, many children do not eat enough fresh fruit, preferring processed varieties often containing extra sugar and fat products.

Prevention

- Reward children with fruit instead of sweets.
- Give them low fat snacks for their break and meals at school.
- Use skimmed or semi-skimmed milk for their cereals.

- Get them out of the house as much as possible by tying in computer games with actual activity games.

- Use an egg timer to limit their use of the computer games.

- Aim for a broad range of food rather than exclusion or severely restricted foods.

- Occasional burgers, sweets and chips are fine so long as they are balanced by other less fattening foods.

Complications

Avoid dieting in children. This may lead to obsessive eating behaviours such as anorexia nervosa and bulimia.

Self-help

Children have the potential to burn off fat through playing active games. It will also pay dividends for later life.

More help

The British Nutrition Foundation gives advice on diet and weight. They also supply helpful leaflets if you provide an SAE. Tel: 020 7404 6504.

Cold sores
Herpes

Herpes is a virus which lives in nerve endings within the skin. It makes its presence felt around the corners of the mouth with crusty, oozing blisters.

Symptoms

- A tingling, itchy feeling is usually felt just before the rash forms.
- Tiny blisters appear, usually at the lips where they join skin.
- The blisters become sore and itchy.
- They then crust over and last about one week before disappearing.
- They can return at any time.

Prevention

There is not a great deal you can do to prevent your child from catching a cold sore other than preventing them from kissing people who have obvious signs of it on their face. You should also ensure that they do not use the same cups or towels as someone who has a cold sore.

Self-help

- Avoid sudden changes in temperature and sun exposure.
- Use simple painkillers such as paracetamol.
- Use a lip salve before they go into bright sunlight.
- Antiviral cream will limit the outbreak.

Colds and flu

Most of us can't tell the difference between a bad cold and flu so you will be delighted to hear that most doctors can't either. The problem with children is that they look so awful when it is just a bad cold. Even so, there are easy and effective ways to treat your child's cold and flu symptoms at home and with medicines from your pharmacy.

How to treat cold and flu symptoms

- Get them to drink plenty of fluids. Hot drinks can have a soothing effect. If they don't feel like eating, try soup instead.

- Use paracetamol (Calpol) according to the instructions (don't give aspirin to a child under twelve years). This will ease their sore throat and muscle aches while bringing their temperature down. Always take the suggested dosage for all medications.

- Do not encourage strenuous exercise but at the same time it is often better if they sit up and watch TV rather than overheating in bed. You can also keep a better eye on them.

- Encourage them to cover their mouth when they cough and sneeze.

- Wash your hands regularly as the virus is passed through skin contact.

- Keep their bedroom well ventilated.

- If they do have flu let them take it easy. Keep them off school for a full recovery.

- Ask your pharmacist for advice. Many infections can be managed effectively with over-the-counter medications. The pharmacist will refer you to your doctor or practice nurse if they think it is necessary.

When to contact your GP

Call your GP's surgery for advice if, after taking over-the-counter medications as directed, your child experiences any of the following:

- symptoms which are severe or unusually prolonged

- shortness of breath

Antibiotics

Some people expect their GP to always give antibiotics to treat children's cold and flu symptoms. Colds and flu are viral illnesses. Antibiotics do not work on viral illness and in fact they can cause more harm than good.

Colic

Typically, attacks start in the evening. Often you will not find any reason for the baby's distressed crying and convulsive movements.

Symptoms

It is most common in two-week-old infants and peaks at about three months. It may be due to an underdeveloped digestive tract, food allergy, wind, not enough sleep or oversensitivity to a busy and noisy home. More likely, it is a combination of them all.

Prevention

- Avoid the swallowing of air by sitting your baby up during feeds.
- Breastfeeding is the best option but watch out if you are drinking too much coffee, tea or other drinks which contain caffeine.
- Too small holes in bottle teats cause your baby to swallow air along with their feed.

Self-help

- Check that your baby is feeding. Hungry babies are not slow to let you know.
- Check that the teat hole is not too small. It should deliver about one drop per second.
- Carry your baby in a sling while you do the housework or sit your baby on top of the washing machine. The rhythmic movement will help lull them to sleep.
- Keep an open mind for serious medical conditions. If you are unsure, always seek medical advice.

More help

Ring NHS Direct or talk to your health visitor.

Conjunctivitis

Inflammation of the transparent covering over the eye, the conjunctiva, is common. Infection, foreign bodies, constant rubbing or chemical irritation are all causes. Children with allergies to plants or certain chemicals may inadvertently cause conjunctivitis by rubbing their eyes after handling the substances. In most cases the inflammation will subside on its own.

Symptoms

The blood vessels in the conjunctiva enlarge and the eye may appear bloodshot. Pus collects during the night under the eyelid and can matt the two eyelids together. Bacterial infections, reactions to chemicals or allergies often affect both eyes whereas viral infections tend only to affect one eye, at least initially. Pus is much less of a feature with allergic or chemical reactions. Instead there can be a quite dramatic swelling of the conjunctiva producing a baggy plastic bag effect around the centre of the eye which remains unaffected. It will settle on its own despite the alarming appearance although it can be treated with anti-inflammatory eye drops.

Causes

Bacteria from another infected person, often a member of the household or a school child, can be passed on through sharing towels or even physical contact. This may also be true for viral infections although they also arise spontaneously. Grass and pollen will irritate the eye, especially if the child suffers from hay fever. Wood resin, household chemicals, petrol, and many other common substances will also cause conjunctivitis.

Prevention

Using separate towels and face cloths while a relation is infected makes good sense.

Complications

Persistent bacterial infection can cause permanent damage to the front of the eye. Viral infections are more serious if they are on the transparent centre of the eye, not the conjunctiva.

Self-help

Bacterial infections need antibacterial drops from your doctor. It can take up to a week for the infection to clear but you can make things much better by gently cleaning the crusted pus away from the eyelids with a soft cloth and warm water. Antihistamine drops make a dramatic difference for allergic conjunctivitis and are available from your pharmacist without a prescription.

More help

If there is any change in your child's vision call your doctor.

Cot death

There can be few more devastating experiences than a cot death in the family. From all the hopes and delight there remains only a crushing emptiness which strains to be filled with all the emotions surrounding the loss. Disbelief and denial are as strong as with any bereavement but guilt is perhaps even stronger. This is all the more sad because in truth we do not know what causes a cot death, but this will not prevent bereaved parents from mercilessly whipping themselves, as if they could somehow have prevented it happening. A blame culture still exists and throwaway remarks about smoking, alcohol or the temperature of the room only serve to reinforce the feeling of misplaced guilt.

Anger is almost as destructive and is often directed at your partner, doctor, housing authorities or all of them at once. Coming to terms with a cot death takes a long time and few people ever really get over it but simply learn how to deal with the feeling of loss. This is a time to be gentle with your partner and yourself.

Some bereaved fathers find counselling helpful while others prefer to handle it on their own. Without doubt the best way of coming to terms with it is to talk to someone who is not judgmental and is quite prepared to listen to the same unanswerable questions over and over again. For men, these gifted people can unfortunately be hard to find and the age-old macho 'pull yourself together' technique is inevitably applied. Give the Foundation for the Study of Infant Deaths a ring or e-mail (see Resources and Contacts). This organisation gives advice and information on preventing cot death and offers support following a bereavement.

Also known as Sudden Infant Death Syndrome (SIDS) the sudden death of infants while in their cots is still a mystery but there are some recognised ways of preventing these tragedies.

Symptoms

One of the most disturbing things about cot death is that generally the baby, usually between three and eighteen months old, has been laid down to sleep with no signs of distress.

Causes

No clearly identifiable cause is known although there are recognised risk factors so it is possible to reduce the possbility of it happening.

Prevention

- Put babies to sleep on their backs, not their faces.

- Do not smoke in the house and encourage others not to do so. If you use a baby minder make sure they understand not to smoke.

- Babies overheat very quickly and will not always make any noise to indicate this. Avoid overheating them by using minimal covers and clothes. If they are hot, cool them with ventilation by taking off their covers and reducing the temperature of the room.

- If you are concerned ring NHS Direct.

- If possible move the cot into your bedroom but avoid sleeping with the baby in your bed.

Self-help

If you have previously lost a baby in this way you should take extra precautions:

- Have your baby weighed and measured regularly.

- Consider buying an apnoea monitor (a device which sets off an alarm if the baby stops breathing).

- Convince your partner and visitors about the danger of smoking in the house.

More help

Talk to your health visitor or doctor.

Coughing

Is the cough worse when people light cigarettes?
YES Passive smoking affects children even if they are not in the same room as you, especially if they have another condition like a cold or asthma. Either smoke outside or give it up.

Does the child have asthma?
YES See 'Asthma'
Coughing is common in asthma. If there are any breathing difficulties, the child cannot speak, the lips are blue or they are not responding to the inhaler, call 999.

Is there also a runny nose, sore throat, fever (the child's temperature is over 38°C/100.4°F) and general aches and pains or sneezing?
YES See 'Colds and Flu'
It is probably a cold or flu. Ask your pharmacist for advice.

Does the child vomit after a bout of coughing with a whooping noise and the child has not been immunised against whooping cough?
YES It could be whooping cough (pertusis). Give paracetamol, put a bowl of water in the room to humidify the air and give them ice lollies. Antibiotics or other medicines have little effect. Call your doctor.

Did a coughing fit start following food such as a peanut or bread going down the wrong way?
YES An obstruction of the airways will cause this kind of coughing. Call 999.

Is there any blood in their phlegm?
YES Repeated coughing can commonly cause small blood vessels to burst but check with your doctor.

Is there also difficulty in breathing or are the lips blue?
YES See 'Asthma'
For whatever reason, the child is not getting enough air. Call 999.

Home treatment

- Give the child extra fluids.
- Avoid a smoky atmosphere.
- Home remedy of one teaspoon of honey in a small glass of warm water sometimes helps.
- Stay with the child in a warm, humid environment such as a bathroom with the shower on.
- If the condition gets worse or new symptoms develop, call your doctor.

Cradle cap

A harmless white/yellow, waxy scale which builds up on the scalp.

Symptoms

A thick white/yellow waxy scale builds up on the scalp. There is no bleeding or obvious irritation unless too vigorous attempts are made to remove it. There is no fever and the child is perfectly well.

Causes

Like many other forms of eczema, the cause is unknown.

Prevention

Routine cleaning will prevent cradle cap in most cases.

Self-help

A form of eczema, it responds well to simply rubbing the affected parts of the scalp with olive oil. Leave it on overnight before washing it off with a mild shampoo in the morning. Anti-dandruff shampoos also help and are available from your pharmacist but you should try rubbing with olive oil first.

More help

See your pharmacist.

Croup

Children between the ages of three months and six years are most likely to suffer from this condition. Croup produces a seal-like barking cough which sounds terrible but is actually rarely serious. The symptoms usually last from three to seven days. As bad luck would have it, the cough is invariably worse during the night.

Causes

Thick mucous at the back of the throat resulting from an initial viral infection.

Prevention

There is no known prevention for croup.

Self-help

It can be treated by steam inhalation and does not need antibiotics. Stay calm. Getting upset will only make matters worse. If you have a bathroom, fill the bath with very hot water so it steams. Alternatively run the shower on full heat with the shower door open. Otherwise choose a room in which it is safe to run a kettle to produce lots of steam. Simply sit with your child allowing them to breathe the warm steam in the room but not directly from the bath, shower or kettle.

Note

Inhaling a peanut or food will produce the same kind of shortness of breath. If your child coughs and has a problem with their breathing while eating take them to your local accident and emergency department.

A serious but now very rare condition called epiglottitis (inflammation of the flap that closes the airway during swallowing) can be confused with croup. There are, however, significant differences in the symptoms. Children with epiglottitis tend to drool while tilting their heads forward. They may have a fever and protrude their jaw as they try to breathe. Epiglottitis is caused by the same bacteria which causes one type of meningitis and has become less common since the introduction of the Hib vaccination.

More help

Ring your doctor.

Crying baby

Is there a rash? `YES` **See 'Rashes'**
Crying is common. If there is a rash as well you need to make sure there is nothing serious going on. Ring your GP.

Is there a fever (your baby has a temperature over 38°C/100.4°F? `YES` **See 'Fever in Children'**
As babies get hot they need to be cooled by taking clothes off them. If this fails to bring their temperature down call your doctor.

Does the crying stop after feeding? `YES` You may need to increase your feeds. Ask your health visitor for advice.

Does the baby cry while feeding on a bottle? `YES` The teat hole may be too small. Try a larger teat hole. Alternatively the baby may have a blocked nose and cannot breathe properly while feeding. Ask your health visitor for advice. Avoid overuse of over-the-counter medicines for coughs which may make things worse.

Does the baby cry after vomiting up all their food after each feed? `YES` **See 'Vomiting in Babies'**
There may be a problem with your baby's stomach. Call your doctor.

Does the crying stop each time you pick up the baby? `YES` **See 'Colic'**
It may be colic. As we don't really know what causes it, things which make the baby feel better are your best bet. Gentle soothing and rocking may help. Get someone else onto the job as well if possible. Discuss the options with your health visitor.

Home treatment

- If you think the child may be hungry, try to give him/her some of his/her normal food.
- You may be able to soothe the child by taking them for a ride in the buggy.
- If the condition gets worse or if any new symptoms develop, call your doctor.

Diarrhoea in babies

Has the diarrhoea occurred more than three times in the last twenty-four hours?	**YES** Babies lose water very quickly through diarrhoea. Call your doctor.
Are you adding sugar to fruit juices or to the bottle feeds?	**YES** Sugar can cause diarrhoea and make existing diarrhoea worse. If the baby is hungry use more feed rather than sugar. Ask your health visitor for advice.
Has the baby just started solid foods?	**YES** It may be too soon for solid foods. Ask your health visitor for advice.
Has the baby just started new medicines?	**YES** Some medicines, such as antibiotics, can cause diarrhoea. Do not stop the medicines. Ask your pharmacist for advice.
Is there a fever (the baby's temperature is over 38°C/100.4°F), vomiting and the baby is not keeping fluids down?	**YES** Call your doctor. If there is also a blue/black rash dial 999 (see 'Meningitis').
Is there blood in the diarrhoea?	**YES** Some infections and obstructions of the bowel can cause bleeding and diarrhoea. Dial 999.

Home treatment

- The majority of diarrhoea is caused through the baby's feed. If breastfeeding, continue to feed on demand.
- Use extra fluids between feeds.
- Bottle-fed babies should be offered as much fluids or rehydration preparations as they demand. If the diarrhoea continues, alternate bottle feeds with rehydration preparations for the next eight hours, then introduce normal feeds.

Earache

Is there itchiness just inside the ear or is the pain worse when the ear lobe is pulled?	**YES**	There may be an infection of the outer part of the ear. Ask your pharmacist for advice.
Is their hearing dull or does it change as they move their head or did the pain come on after a bath or swimming?	**YES**	There may be wax against the ear drum with water held inside the ear causing hearing dullness and pain. Ask your pharmacist for advice.
Is the pain very severe or is there vomiting or a yellow discharge from the ear?	**YES**	**See 'Middle Ear Infection'** There may be an infection of the middle ear. Call your doctor.
Is there also pain in the teeth or jaw?	**YES**	They may have a dental abscess or bad tooth. Call your dentist.
Do they have a cold or hay fever?	**YES**	**See 'Colds and Flu'** The tube which connects the back of the ear to the throat keeps the pressure the same on both sides. It gets blocked during a cold. Tell them to try swallowing hard while holding their nose. Your pharmacist will advise on decongestants.
Did the pain come on during or after a plane trip?	**YES**	There may have been unequal pressure on each side of the eardrum. This happens more often when they have a cold or an ear infection. Tell them to try swallowing hard while holding their nose. Give paracetamol. If the pain does not go away after two days speak to your doctor.
Did the pain come on after trying to clean out wax with their finger or some object?	**YES**	They may have damaged the sensitive lining of the ear or even the eardrum itself. Ask your doctor for advice. The smallest thing they should put in their ear is their elbow! Never use cotton buds to clear wax as they only push the wax further in and may cause damage to the inside of their ear.
Has the child got tender lumps behind the ear?	**YES**	Some infections can travel into the bone around the ear. Call your doctor.

Home treatment

- If you cannot sort out what to do from this list phone your doctor.

Eating disorders

Children, like adults, will experience short-term eating problems. It is only when the problem is prolonged and affects their behaviour that action should be taken as it can have serious consequences for their health. Although there are some factors which seem to trigger the disorders, it is impossible to predict which children will experience eating problems or what form they will take. Some children will refuse to eat at all, while others will binge food only to force vomiting later on. It is seen most in teenage and young adult women although increasingly eating disorders are affecting young men as well: up to 10 per cent of eating disorders are amongst men. Although showing itself as an obsession with body image, weight and eating, these disorders may be triggered by problems over which children have little control, such as sexual persuasion, chronic disease, family strife or school pressure.

Symptoms

- continual weight checking or examination in a mirror
- irrational fear of gaining weight or looking overweight
- binge eating followed by forced vomiting and fasting
- laxative and water tablet abuse without any apparent need
- compulsive exercise
- secret eating of the same kind of food, especially cakes or sweet food
- hoarding secret supplies of food
- stealing food from friends or shops
- late onset of menstruation or it stopping after having already started
- poor insight into real body image with a constant perception of being grossly overweight

Causes

- lack of self-esteem
- bullying

- parental pressure to diet
- depression and anxiety are linked but it can be difficult to tell which comes first
- solvent, alcohol or drug abuse are also linked
- media and peer pressure

Prevention

- never put children on a diet unless medically advised to do so (see 'Childhood Obesity')
- be prepared to talk through their concerns and show there are ways of coping with them
- aim for containing the problem if it has occurred and then move on to improve things
- being judgemental will make things worse

Complications

Eating disorders can be life-threatening or can damage the physical and mental development of children. Tragically, suicide is also higher in children with eating disorders.

Self-help

Expert medical help is often needed but you can most help your child by supporting them.

- avoid talk of diets and weight loss
- be honest about your own feelings without being angry
- avoid unloading your worries on them and, in a way, reversing roles
- life must go on so try not to allow the eating disorder to disrupt the family's everyday activities.
- involve the child in planning the next day's meal

More help

Eating Disorders Association (EDA)
Helpline: 01603 621 414
Youthline: 01603 765 050

Eczema

Basically eczema is inflammation of the skin, for whatever reason or cause, which produces dry flaky skin, more often on the inside of joints such as the elbow. It is more common in young children.

The term dermatitis is exactly the same thing but tends to be used when the eczema is caused by contact with a chemical or other substances.

Symptoms

Atopic eczema is an allergic condition. Children who suffer from other allergies such as hay fever are also prone to eczema. It can affect any part of the body but the flexures of joints, inside the elbows, knees, and wrists are the most common sites. The dry flaky skin can come and go but tends to be worse in winter or cold weather.

Contact dermatitis can be very severe with the skin becoming deeply inflamed leading to skin loss. The underlying deep skin looks red and angry. Infection is often the next step. Seborrhoeic dermatitis may be fungal in origin, although it could equally be an extreme form of allergy affecting the hairy parts of the body.

Seborrhoeic dermatitis predominately affects the scalp and eyebrows. A thick yellow greasy scale builds up leading to heavy dandruff.

Causes

Atopic eczema is probably an inherited condition. The inflammation flares up as a response to some allergy although it may never be identified.

Washing powders are known to cause contact dermatitis in susceptible children.

Prevention

It makes sense to identify and avoid those substances, materials or chemicals which trigger the eczema.

- keep the skin moist with emollients (e.g. E45 cream)
- use a bathwater additive which contains moisturising oils

Complications

Secondary infection may occur, especially in very young children. Unfortunately, topical steroid creams, which can be so effective in the treatment of eczema, also make the skin more prone to infection.

Contact dermatitis can be so severe that the skin is lost in the affected area leading to infection and scarring. Not surprisingly this can be both intensely itchy and painful.

Self-help

There is a wide range of products which will help to stop the itchiness and keep the skin moist. Topical steroid creams may be helpful but given the potential side effects, these should be used with care. Seek advice from your GP.

Scratching and itchiness can be reduced by keeping the skin moist and taking antihistamine tablets or medicine. This is useful for young children as antihistamines have a mild sedative effect making for a better night's sleep for everyone.

More help

Speak to your doctor especially if:

- the eczema is spreading
- the skin is infected
- there is severe pain

Febrile convulsions

These are essentially fits caused by high body temperature. They do not mean that your child will continue to have fits for the rest of their lives.

Symptoms

- slight to violent shaking
- drowsiness afterwards
- incontinence
- high temperature
- confusion before and afterwards

Causes

- High fevers are the most common cause of fits in children aged six months to four years.
- Any illness causing a temperature higher than 39°C (102°F) can set off a febrile convulsion.
- Other causes of convulsions include poisons, infections, reactions to medications and, very rarely, vaccinations.

Prevention

- Remove all heavy clothing; a tee-shirt or pyjama top will do.
- Sponge the child down with lukewarm water and give paracetamol according to the bottle instructions.
- Continue trying to reduce fever in this way until it is 38.5°C (101°F) or less.
- Give the child ice lollies to suck on.

Complications

- choking on vomit
- physical harm from hitting something hard during the fit

Self-help

Do not restrain a child suffering from a febrile convulsion. Simply protect them from hard objects and continue to lower any high temperature by tepid sponging only. If a child is suffering from a convusion

- roll the child on his or side (see 'Emergency First Aid', p. 99)
- give nothing by mouth until they have completely recovered from the fit
- give your child rectal diazepam if told to by your doctor

More help

Although you should call your doctor if your child has a fit, less than half of the children who have a fit will ever have another one. Call 999 if there is any choking, the fits continue or there is any sign of meningitis (see 'Meningitis').

Fever in children

Does the child have a temperature over 38°C/100.4°F?

YES Try and lower the child's temperature with paracetamol, not aprin. Keep the child in a cool room wearing little clothing. Call your doctor if their temperature is not falling or if their general condition deteriorates.

Are there any tender swellings around the jaw and neck and has the child been immunised against mumps?

YES It is probably swollen glands. Give the child paracetamol and ask your pharmacist for advice. If it continues for two weeks, speak to your doctor.

Is there also earache?

YES **See 'Earache'**
Middle ear infections may be the culprit. Call your doctor and give paracetamol to ease the pain.

Is there a sore throat or sneezing or a cough or a runny nose?

YES **See 'Colds'**
It is probably a cold or flu. Ask your pharmacist for advice.

Is there also diarrhoea?

YES **See 'Diarrhoea in Babies'**
Babies and children lose water very quickly. Call your doctor.

Is there any difficulty breathing?

YES **See 'Allergies' and 'Asthma'**
Any difficulty in breathing in children for whatever cause needs medical attention. Call your doctor.

Is there pain in the abdomen?

YES **See 'Abdominal Pain'**
There are a whole stack of reasons why children will have abdominal pain and thankfully most of them are not serious.

Is the child difficult to wake, not taking or keeping down fluids or complaining of the light hurting their eyes?

YES **See 'Meningitis'**
As it can difficult to be sure whether you are dealing with something simple or serious you should ring your doctor.

Is there a rash?

YES **See 'Rashes'**
Rashes often accompany a fever.

Home treatment

- Give the child regular paracetamol to reduce the temperature (check the instructions on the packet for the right dose).
- Give them an extra amount of their favourite drink or ice lollies.
- Make sure the child is not overdressed – a vest and nappy/pants is enough clothing for them as long as the house is at the normal room temperature.
- Cover the child in a light cotton sheet when in bed.
- If the condition gets worse or new symptoms develop, call your doctor.

German measles
Rubella

Now uncommon thanks to the MMR vaccine
(see 'Immunisation').

Symptoms

The child is rarely ill but will have a mildly raised temperature
and swollen glands on the neck and base of the skull.

The pinhead-sized flat red spots last around two days and
need no treatment other than some paracetamol for the slight
fever.

Causes

The virus is very contagious and will spread quickly in a
population which is not immune.

Prevention

The MMR vaccination is both safe and effective for girls and
boys.

Complications

Very rarely the virus that causes German measles will cause an
inflammation of the brain (encephalitis).

The real danger may come in later life if an unvaccinated
woman becomes infected with German measles while pregnant.
For this major reason alone both boys and girls should be
immunised.

Self-help

Paracetamol will reduce the mild fever.

Glue ear
Secretory otitis media

Found only in young children, glue ear was once thought to be an infection, which it isn't, and that antibiotics would help, which they don't. As the presence of the jelly-like substance within the middle ear probably caused some hearing loss it seemed sensible to remove it and allow it to drain freely through a small plastic pipe placed in the eardrum. Fewer doctors are now convinced that this is such a good idea after all and like tonsillectomies, there are far less operations taking place. Even so, many children suffer significant hearing loss from glue ear just at the age when school work and language development is so important.

Symptoms

There is no pain but the child may complain of a dull feeling in their ear. Hearing loss is very variable and can fluctuate. It is often their teacher who notices the problem after first putting it down to simply lack of attention in class.

Causes

The cause is unknown although the shorter more horizontal Eustachian tube in young children may be a factor because it blocks more easily. There is no hard evidence that glue ear causes permanent hearing loss.

Complications

The main concern is that glue ear will possibly interfere with the child's education and language development.

Self-help

If you suspect glue ear, ring your doctor. Paying particular attention to any hearing difficulties while the condition settles or until the child is treated surgically is most important.

Head injury

Is the child unconscious? | **YES** | If the injury was only to the head, lie them on one side, with a cushion at their back, upper knee brought forward, head pointing downward to allow any vomit to escape without being inhaled. If there is any danger of neck injury or spine injury do not move them. Call 999.

Did the child become unconscious or difficult to rouse immediately after the injury? | **YES** | Any loss of consciousness needs to be checked. Call 999.

Are they deaf in one ear or are they seeing double? | **YES** | There may be a skull fracture or an internal skull injury. Call 999.

Have they vomited more than twice since the accident? | **YES** | Head injuries do tend to make children vomit but they should stop soon afterwards. If the vomiting comes on later, or more than twice, take them to accident and emergency.

Are they increasingly difficult to rouse afterwards as time passes? | **YES** | Children do tend to sleep after a head injury. This is fine so long as you can rouse them every hour for the first six hours after the injury or they are not vomiting. Otherwise call NHS Direct or take them to the accident and emergency department.

Has there been any fit, turn or convulsion immediately after the injury or at any time since? | **YES** | Any fit should be checked out. Call 999.

Home treatment

- Place a cold face cloth over the bruised area.
- Give the child paracetamol if you think they are in pain – read the instructions for the correct dose.
- Encourage the child to rest quietly for the next forty-eight hours and observe for signs of deterioration. This may include frequent bouts of sickness and abnormal behaviour.
- If any other symptoms develop call NHS Direct or your GP.

Hives
Urticaria

Hives are small, often itchy, raised red spots which you can feel and which are rarely serious unless combined with any breathing problems.

The rash will usually disappear in a few hours without any treatment.

Causes

It is most often caused by a viral infection but may be caused by certain foods and plants, such as nettles.

Complications

In rare cases the rash may become severe and is accompanied by breathing difficulties. This is an emergency. Call 999.

Self-help

Antihistamine creams and antihistamine medicine may help. Ask your pharmacist.

More help

If there is any shortness of breath call 999.

Immunisation timetable

MMR: the big issue

Deciding whether or not to immunise your children can be worrying stuff. There is no shortage of press coverage of children with brain damage, autism or Crohn's disease which have resulted from some form of immunisation. It would be dishonest to say that there is absolutely no risk from any form of vaccination but the hype often fails to mention that infectious diseases like polio were once the greatest cause of death for our children. Yes, better living conditions have played a part in their prevention but so have vaccination

Age: 2 months	Age: 3 months	Age: 4 months
Immunisation Diphtheria, tetanus, whooping cough (Pertussis) Hib **Type** One injection (first dose) **Common side effects** Possible small lump at injection site. Slightly raised temperature. Possible risk of fit from higher temperatures.	**Immunisation** Diphtheria, tetanus, whooping cough (Pertussis) Hib **Type** One injection (second dose) **Common side effects** As for 2 months	**Immunisation** Diphtheria, tetanus, whooping cough (Pertussis) Hib **Type** One injection (third dose) **Common side effects** As for 2 months
Polio **Type** By mouth (first dose) **Common side effects** None	**Polio** **Type** One injection (second dose) **Common side effects** None	**Polio** **Type** By mouth (third dose) **Common side effects** None
Meningitis (Hib (Haemophilius Influenzae type b) and Meningococcal Group C) **Type:** Injection **Common side effects** Local injection site irritation	**Meningitis (Hib (Haemophilius Influenzae type b) and Meningococcal Group C)** **Type:** Injection **Common side effects** Local injection site irritation	**Meningitis (Hib (Haemophilius Influenzae type b) and Meningococcal Group C)** **Type:** Injection **Common side effects:** Local injection site irritation

programmes. Measles, for instance, is a nasty infection and can cause a potentially lethal inflamation of the brain; mumps can cause infertility; and rubella (German measles) can cause dreadful birth defects for the unborn child. As yet there is no scientifically proven evidence that the combined MMR vaccine causes autism or Crohn's disease, despite extensive research. You can ask for the single vaccination but it is not as effective as the combined version and subjects the child to more injections. It is your choice, and unlike in some parts of the world, there is no form of coercion. At the time of writing there is a steady rise in the number of cases of measles, where before GPs rarely ever saw a single case.

Age: 12–15 months	Age: 4–5 years	Age: 10–14 years
Immunisation **Measles, mumps, rubella (German measles) MMR** **Type:** One injection **Common side effects** High temperatures and measles like rash which is not infectious. Small risk of temperature causing a febrile convulsion.	**Immunisation** **Measles, mumps, rubella (German measles) MMR** **Type:** One injection (booster) **Common side effects** As at 12–15 months but less common	**Immunisation** BCG (tuberculosis) **Type:** Skin test plus injection if required **Common side effects** Irritation and pain at injection site. Blister or sore which may leave a small scar.
	Diphtheria, tetanus **Type:** One injection (booster) **Common side effects:** Possible small lump at injection site. Slight temperature rise.	
	Polio **Type:** By mouth (booster) **Common side effects** None	

Impetigo

Bacterial infections of the skin are fairly common. Impetigo is more common in children but is also seen in adults. It is infectious but is no longer a serious threat, thanks to antibiotics.

Symptoms

- It usually starts as a small red spot which gradually increases in size.

- The top becomes crusty and weeps.

- It is often found around the corners of the mouth and face, but can also be found on the rest of the body.

Causes

A bacterial infection that is picked up through contact with an infected child.

Prevention

Use individual washing materials during the course of the infection.

Complications

It will spread more quickly in children who are run down with an illness and on strong steroids.

Self-help

Clean the spots with a damp tissue and discard it so as not to spread the infection. Give paracetamol for pain relief.

Insect bites and stings

At first you may mistake the marks as something more serious.

Symptoms

Looking very closely, you may be able to see the small hole of the bite. The spot is invariably itchy and may swell particularly if it came from a horsefly (cleg).

Causes

Midges, horseflies, bees, wasps, centipedes, ants and so forth – the list is long but thankfully there are no killers in the UK.

Prevention

Insect repellents work. Use a mosquito net around the bed when in infested areas, particularly for children.

Complications

Some children are strongly allergic to bites and stings and can be very ill. If there is any shortage of breath, dial 999. Bites can become infected by scratching.

Self-help

Although itchy and sometimes painful they are rarely dangerous and need only some antihistamine or local anaesthetic cream from your pharmacist.

Lice

These tiny parasites can live on any hairy bits of the body. Female lice lay eggs every day. These hatch in eight to ten days.

Symptoms

Nearly always they are completely harmless, but terribly itchy. Lice and their eggs (nits) can be seen on the hair shafts.

Causes

Lice are very common amongst children and infestation has nothing to do with dirty living.

Prevention

- Lice are easily caught from others. Avoid spreading lice by treating the whole family even when only one person is infected.

- Avoid lending or borrowing hats, brushes or combs.

- Keep hair clean.

As nits can stay alive for two days when they are not on a human being, make sure that clothes and hats which have been worn, as well as combs and brushes, are thoroughly cleaned.

Self-help

- Comb the hair regularly while wet with a fine-toothed comb. Use a conditioner.

- Ask your pharmacist for the most suitable lotion. There will be a local policy on the treatment of head lice.

The safest and most effective treatment is daily combing with a nit comb after washing the hair with conditioner.

More help

Community Hygiene Concern (CHC), a government-funded organisation, supplies leaflets on 'bug busting'.
CHC Helpline: 020 8341 7167

Measles

Children are most vulnerable to this highly contagious viral infection. With widespread uptake of the MMR vaccine it is now very rare.

Symptoms

Symptoms usually develop in a well-established order:

- a mild to severe temperature of around 39°C/102.2°F
- tiredness and general fatigue
- poor appetite
- running nose and sneezing
- irritable dry cough
- red eyes and sensitivity to light
- tiny white spots in the mouth and throat
- a blotchy red rash that starts behind the ears, spreads to the face and then to the rest of the body and lasts for up to seven days

Causes

It takes between ten and twelve days for the virus to make its presence felt after infection from another child. Physical contact, sneezing and clothing contaminated with nasal secretions all help to spread this infection.

Prevention

Although immunisation rates are now very high you should isolate your child from other children if you think they may be infected. Immunised children and those who have already caught measles are virtually immune.

Complications

Meningitis and pneumonia are rare, but serious, complications. More commonly, eyes and ears develop secondary infections which may need antibiotics from your doctor.

Self-help

Once the rash starts it is a matter of treating the symptoms.

- Check the child's temperature.

- Use paracetamol elixir (Calpol/Disprol) for fever, aches and pains.

- Light sensitivity can be helped by reducing sunlight or electric lights in the room.

- Use a ball of damp cotton wool to clean away any crustiness around the eyes.

- Cough medicines are of little value but do ease ticklish throats. Try placing a bowl of water in the room.

- Avoid dehydration. Feverish small children rapidly lose water. It also makes a cough worse.

- Give the child one teaspoon of lemon juice and two teaspoons of honey in a glass of warm water.

- Ideally, you should keep your child away from others for at least seven days after the start of the rash.

After four days the child usually feels better.

More help

Vaccinate your children against measles (see 'Immunisation').

Meningitis/Septicaemia

A rare illness, meningitis causes inflammation of the brain lining which can be fatal. Viral infections are usually less severe than those caused by bacteria. Unfortunately the symptoms can easily be mistaken for flu or a bad cold. Worse still it is more difficult to be certain with babies and young children. If you are not sure, you must call NHS Direct. Continued immunisation against Hib (bacterial) meningitis looks set to eliminate this type of meningitis from our community.

Symptoms

Babies under two years:

- they can be difficult to wake

- their cry may be high-pitched and different from normal

- they may vomit repeatedly, not just after feeds

- they refuse feeds, either from the bottle, breast or by spoon

- their skin may appear pale or blotchy, possibly with blue/black stains which don't go white when you press your finger or a glass tumbler on them

- the soft spot on top of your baby's head (the fontanelle) may be tight or bulging

- the baby moans when you lift its legs to change a nappy

Remember a fever may not be present in the early stages.

Older children may have slightly different symptoms:

- a constant generalised headache

- a high temperature

- vomiting

- drowsiness

- confusion

- sensitivity to bright lights, daylight or even the TV

- neck stiffness – moving their chin to their chest will be very painful

- rash of red/blue spots or bruises which don't go white when pressed with a glass tumbler; the rash may not be present in the early stages

Causes

There are different types of meningitis which can be caused by either bacteria or viruses.

Prevention

Vaccination is now available for Meningitis C. It is safe and extremely effective. Some forms of meningitis do not, as yet, have a vaccination so the disease can still occur. It pays to be vigilant.

More help

The National Meningitis Trust provides free information to sufferers of meningitis and their relatives. There is also a 24-hour support line: 0345 538118.

People who have been in contact with someone who has had meningitis should contact the next of kin of the patient to find out any instructions (from the hospital or the director of public health) that they may have been given. Otherwise your doctor will be able to give you appropriate advice. Only those who have been in very close contact with the infected person are given antibiotics and vaccination. Call 999.

Middle ear infection
Acute otitis media

Infections of the middle ear are common, particularly in children. Various theories attempt to explain this but we do know that the infections are not as serious as once thought. Even so, they are very painful and can cause a temporary loss of hearing. A recent cold or throat infection may have happened before the pain in the ear started.

Symptoms

Most children complain of a dullness in their hearing as if there was cotton wool blocking their ear. There is also a severe throbbing pain made worse sometimes by coughing. If there is pus behind the eardrum it may leak through a small hole, not unlike a boil on the skin. Once the pus escapes the pain rapidly declines. It is difficult not to notice this happening as the pus usually flows out very quickly and has a strong smell. The eardrum repairs itself with time and there is very rarely any permanent loss of hearing as a result.

Causes

Children are thought by some people to suffer more from middle ear infections because the tube which connects the ear to the back of the throat – the Eustachian tube – is shorter and more horizontal than in adults so bacteria is more likely to pass into the ear. Not all agree, but the tube usually does block when infected and as its job is to keep pressure equal on both sides of the eardrum, the blockage produces a build-up in the middle ear, which is the main cause of pain.

Prevention

Some doctors feel that mentholated pastilles sucked during a cold may prevent the Eustachian tube from blocking but there is no hard evidence to support this.

Complications

It was once thought that middle ear infections caused permanent loss of hearing. This is no longer considered completely true. In the past serious infections of the skull bones next to the middle ear (mastoiditis) were dangerous and often led to complete deafness in that ear. Thankfully it is now very rare although we do not know why.

Self-help

Pain relief is the main treatment as antibiotics take a long time to have an effect and may not be of any real value. Paracetamol will reduce the pain and hard swallowing should be encouraged rather than blowing against a pinched nose to help unblock the Eustachian tube.

More help

If the pain persists call your doctor.

Nappy rash

Nappy rashes are common but can be reduced in severity or avoided completely.

Symptoms

The rash is usually red, not raised and confined to the nappy area.

Causes

It is caused by the irritating effect of urine and motions. If they are cleaned away quickly enough, or if the baby is allowed to have the nappy off for a while, the rash will not appear.

Prevention

- As far as is possible, change each nappy following soiling. Remember that urine can be every bit as irritating as faeces.

- Avoid disposable wipes containing alcohol or moisturising chemicals. Instead use plenty of warm water.

- As much as is practical, leave the nappy and any plastic pants off. Dry, cool skin rarely forms a nappy rash.

- Reusable nappies should be washed as directed by the manufacturer. Avoid caustic household detergents.

Complications

An angry red rash which does not respond or extends beyond the nappy area may be a fungal infection (candida). You need an anti-fungal cream and an oral anti-fungal agent. Ask your pharmacist or doctor.

Self-help

Promptly treat any rash appearing with ointment from your pharmacist. Avoid talcum powder which can cake badly and cause even more irritation.

Nosebleeds

Nosebleeds are common in children. The vast majority are spontaneous, often following a cold or chest infection. In very rare cases they can be caused by a blood disorder.

Symptoms

Nosebleeds can look quite dramatic but they are rarely serious. They are generally painless and from only one nostril. Although it looks as though the child is losing a large amount of blood it is actually very small.

Causes

The blood vessels in the nose are very close to the surface. At one place inside the nose a number of blood vessels meet and bleeding from this area – Little's area – is common.

Prevention

As there is generally no warning it is difficult to prevent a nosebleed. Cautery – burning the blood vessels – by a surgeon does help but if a child is prone to nosebleeds they may well recur.

Self-help

Tell the child to avoid swallowing the blood as it irritates the stomach and will make them vomit. Tip their head forward over a sink or basin, firmly pinch the soft part of the nose just in front of the bridge and allow the blood to run out of their mouth. The bleeding will stop in around ten to fifteen minutes. Once it has stopped tell your child not to blow their nose and not to cough for the next eight to ten hours to avoid starting a fresh bleed.

More help

If the bleeding fails to stop or if your child is suffering from repeated nosebleeds you need to call your doctor.

Poisoning

Is the poison household bleach or petrol?

YES Do not try to make them sick. Give them small sips of milk and stay calm. Most poisons such as bleach or petrol only go as far as the mouth. Call 999.

Is the poison some sort of medicine the child has got hold of or has been given too much of?

YES Do not try to make them sick. Take any containers of medicines they may have taken with you to the hospital. Call 999.

Is the child very drowsy or unconscious?

YES Lie them on their side, with a cushion behind their back and their upper leg pulled slightly forward so they don't fall on their face or roll backwards. Wipe any vomit away from their mouth. Keep the head pointing downward to allow any vomit to escape without being breathed in. Call 999.

Is it possible for children to get hold of poisons or medicines in the house, garage or shed?

YES Lock all chemical and medicines away in a child-proof container. Always keep them in their original containers. Never put chemicals such as weedkiller in soft drink bottles. Ask the Royal Society for the Prevention of Accidents (Tel: 0121 248 2000) for advice about avoiding accidents such as this happening.

Home treatment

- If you cannot sort out what to do from this list please phone NHS Direct or your GP.

Rashes

All babies and children will have a rash at some time (sometimes called 'heat rash').

Symptoms

It looks like a fine pattern of tiny red spots which come and go but tend to disappear if their temperature is lowered. The baby will be perfectly well although they may be drowsy or crying from the heat.

Causes

A cold or a viral infection are the most common causes. Too many clothes or bedding will also cause it.

Complications

If your baby gets too hot they may have a fit (febrile convulsion). Cool them down immediately by removing their clothes and keep them in a cool room.

Self-help

No treatment is required other than lowering their temperature with paracetamol syrup. Ask your pharmacist for advice.

More help

Call your doctor if they have a febrile convulsion (see 'Febrile Convulsions').

Ringworm
Tinea

Ringworm can affect many parts of the body, particularly the groin and scalp.

Symptoms

It is most noticeable on bare skin and is referred to as ringworm due to its characteristic appearance as a circular patch of red, itchy skin, which gradually increases in size. There may also be red itchy areas around the base of hair shafts. With scratching, these areas can bleed and become crusted with blood.

Causes

It is not a worm as the name suggests. It is a fungus.

Prevention

Use a separate face cloth and towel – ringworm is infectious.

Complications

Bacterial infection from scratching is common.

Self-help

- Keep the area well ventilated and dry.
- Use an antifungal cream or shampoo – available from your pharmacist.

More help

See your pharmacist or doctor.

Scabies

Although intensely itchy, scabies is rarely a serious condition.

Symptoms

Red lines which follow the burrows of the mite as it travels in the skin soon merge with the inevitable scratching. It is usually worse at night when the mite is most active.

Causes

Scabies is caused by a mite which burrows just under the skin, often between the fingers, on wrists, elbows and the genital areas and causes a red rash. It can only come from contact with infected people.

Prevention

It is very difficult to prevent. Making your child wear gloves all day is not a reasonable option.

Complications

Bacterial infection from scratching can make things worse.

Self-help

Ointments are available from your pharmacist. The whole body will need to be covered with the ointment for twenty-four hours and all clothing and bedding should be washed thoroughly.

More help

See your pharmacist.

Sore mouth

Are there spots or discoloured patches inside the mouth?

`YES` If they are creamy yellow and scrape off leaving a raw area it may be a thrush infection. If they do not scrape off they are probably mouth ulcers. See your doctor.

Are the gums red, swollen and painful?

`YES` There may be a gum infection. Bad breath is often present as well. Check with your dentist.

Is the pain and spots/rash only at the lips?

`YES` **See 'Cold Sores'**
If the rash is at the junction between lip and skin it is probably a cold sore (herpes). See your pharmacist.

Are there painful cracks at the corners of the mouth?

`YES` In children it is often caused by constant licking at the edges of their mouths. See your pharmacist.

Is the pain worse when biting down or is it located in one tooth?

`YES` **See 'Toothache'**
It may be an abscess or bad tooth. See your dentist.

Home treatment

- If you are still not sure check with your dentist.

Sore throats

Is there also sneezing, a runny nose and a cough?

YES See 'Colds and Flu'
It is probably a cold. Ask your pharmacist for advice.

Has this been going on for more than two weeks or is their voice now hoarse?

YES Any prolonged throat soreness, difficulty in swallowing or voice hoarseness needs to be checked out. Speak to your doctor.

Are the tonsils speckled white or do they have pus on them (the tonsils are the floppy red flaps at each side of the back of the throat, not the single flap hanging down in the middle)?

YES See 'Tonsillitis'
It could be tonsillitis or pharyngitis. Try letting them gargle with aspirin (not for those under twelve years) or soothing with throat lozenges. Call your doctor.

Are there any tender lumps just in front of the ear at the angle of the jaw?

YES These could be swollen lymph glands which are common with sore throats. Give paracetamol to ease the pain.

Is there a fever (the temperature is over 38°C/100.4°F)?

YES See 'Fever in Children'
If they also have a general feeling of being unwell, a cough and a headache they probably have a viral infection which will settle on its own. Give paracetamol but if it is not settling call your doctor.

Is it impossible for them to swallow their own saliva?

YES If their throat is so swollen they need immediate medical advice. Call 999.

Styes

Boils can form wherever there are hairs growing. This includes the eyelids which can develop a staphylococcus infection next to an eyelash. Despite its dreadful appearance, it is still only a boil and will rarely cause any long-term problem.

Symptoms

A red lump first appears at the edge of the eyelid. This becomes more painful as it swells in size. After a couple of days a head forms just as with a boil elsewhere on the skin. Soon afterwards the stye will burst and the pain disappear.

Causes

Like any other boil they just happen. If children are getting boils on a regular basis you should have it checked out as conditions like diabetes make them more susceptible to boils and styes.

Prevention

There is no way of preventing a stye.

Complications

In the past people were quite aggressive about dealing with styes and would even cut into the lid margin allowing it to drain. There was a real danger of scarring by scratching the eye each time the person blinked. This is now very rare.

Self-help

Compresses made from clean white cotton cloth soaked in warm water and pressed against the stye are painful but do help bring the stye to a head. Some people then advise removing the eyelash next to the stye allowing the pus to drain. This doesn't always work and can be very painful. The stye will burst on its own, often during sleep.

More help

Antibiotics are not usually of great value as the stye will disappear on its own. Call your doctor if they keep coming back.

Teething problems

Your baby's first teeth to appear will be the front incisors and they don't usually give much bother to the child in his or her first year. Although there is considerable variation between babies the times of teething average out as follows:

six months – first incisors (front teeth)

seven months – second incisors

twelve months – first molars (back teeth)

eighteen months – canines (eye teeth)

two to three years – second molars

A full set of teeth for children over three years is twenty.

Symptoms

Inflammation of the gums with more dribbling than usual is generally accompanied by chewing fingers or anything else such as teething rings that comes along.

Causes

First and second molars usually come through between one and three years of age and are much more likely to cause pain. Hot cheeks, tender gums and irritability are all common during this time.

Prevention

Letting them chew early can help.

Self-help

Cool teething rings, cool drinks and gently rubbing the gums can all help ease the pain. Some people also swear by homeopathic and herbal remedies. Excessive use of local anaesthetic gels is not helpful in the long run as they stem the chewing and it is the action of chewing which allows the teeth to cut through. My dad swore by rubbing my gums with his calloused finger – he was a moulder – after first dipping it in whiskey. This explains a great deal.

More help

Other conditions such as ear infections can be mistaken for teething and if your baby will not settle or has a high temperature you should ring NHS Direct or your GP.

Tonsillitis

Most sore throats will settle themselves within a few days and do not need antibiotics. The tonsils sit at each side of the back of the throat. The red wobbly thing hanging down in the middle is not a tonsil.

Symptoms

- varying degrees of throat or ear pain
- swollen glands on either side of the neck or jaw
- difficulty in swallowing

Causes

Sore throats are horribly common. Most are caused by viruses. There are thankfully few serious throat infections, although diphtheria, a severe throat infection, is only kept under control by vaccination. Tonsillitis simply means an inflammation of the tonsils, which may be caused by a bacterial or viral infection.

Prevention

There is no prevention.

Complications

Call your doctor if the child:

- cannot even swallow fluids
- is drooling and unable to swallow their saliva
- shows any of the signs of meningitis (see 'Meningitis')
- is having any difficulty breathing
- has a persistent temperature over 38°C/100.4°F

Self-help

- Give them ice lollies or ice cream to cool the tonsils.

- Make them gargle with warm salt water (one teaspoon in a glass of water) every four hours or so.

- Avoid acid drinks or spicy food.

- Use soothing lozenges – avoid the medicated variety. For very young children ask your pharmacist.

- Paracetamol elixirs can work wonders particularly before bedtime. For very young children ask your pharmacist.

A tonsillectomy is only needed with repeated infections or an abscess. Despite the enormous size of tonsils, most children will still be able to swallow food. It is quite normal for young children to have very large tonsils but cause no problems. Children's tonsils were once removed quicker than you could say 'Ah'. Now we recognise their value as part of the body's defence system.

More help

Call your doctor.

Toothache

Is the pain severe, continuous and is there no relief with paracetamol?

YES They probably have an abscess beneath the tooth. Call your dentist.

Does the pain come and go and is it made worse by biting down on the tooth?

YES They probably have decay inside one of their teeth. Make an appointment with your dentist.

Have they recently had a tooth filled by your dentist?

YES Pain is common, even for up to a week afterwards. Ask your pharmacist for advice. If the pain lasts longer than a week, call your dentist.

Is there also pain in the front of their face made worse with coughing?

YES They may have sinusitis, an infection of the spaces in the bones of the face. Give them paracetamol and ring your doctor.

Is there a foul smell in their mouth?

YES **See 'Sore Mouth'**
Halitosis, smelly breath, is a common result of a tooth abscess. See your dentist.

Vomiting in babies

Is there a persistent cough or runny nose?

YES **See 'Colds and Flu'**
Repeated coughing along with a fever is common with colds and flu and will make the baby vomit.

Is there any fever (the baby's temperature is over 38°C/100.4°F)?

YES **See 'Fever in Children'**
High temperatures can cause vomiting in babies and children. Check out the section on fever in children but if your child is obviously unwell ring NHS Direct or your GP.

Are there frequent and very loose bowel motions (more than three in twenty-four hours) as well as the vomiting?

YES Babies dehydrate very quickly. Call your GP.

Is the vomiting forceful (projectile) and after each feed or is there weight loss?

YES There may be a problem with the emptying of the stomach. Call NHS Direct or your GP.

Is the vomiting just small amounts after feeds?

YES Babies often bring up small amounts of their feed but it should look similar to their milk feed and not come out with any force. Winding helps. Using an over-large hole in the teat when bottle-feeding is a common cause. Avoid overuse of colic treatments.

Is the baby crying or moaning continuously or is it obviously in pain?

YES It can be difficult to tell if a baby is in severe pain when it is vomiting. A change in the way the baby is crying, particularly when previously well, or if there is a rash or fever, needs to be checked out by your doctor.

Home treatment

- If breastfeeding, continue as normal, unless vomiting has occurred more than twice, in which case call NHS Direct.

- If bottle-feeding, introduce rehydration fluids, such as Dioralyte, in small quantities.

- Do not give large amounts of fluids at once.

- If the condition has not improved within two hours or if the baby does not have a wet nappy or if other symptoms have developed, call your doctor.

Vomiting in children

Is there also a fever (the child's temperature is over 38°C/100.4°F)?

`YES` **See 'Fever in Children'**
Vomiting is common in children with high temperatures (over 38°C/100.4°F) and simply lowering their temperature with paracetamol tablets (or liquid paracetamol like Calpol) will help.

Has there been vomiting for more than two days?

`YES` Try just giving fluids rather than solid food but if the child is not taking fluids or is bringing most or all of it up, call your doctor.

Is there also diarrhoea or very loose bowel motions?

`YES` It may be gastroenteritis or food poisoning. Call your doctor if you are not sure. Be prepared to tell the doctor the child's age, the name of any medicines they might be taking, any vomiting affecting the rest of the family, any previous medical problems, any food or drink taken which you suspect.

Is there severe pain?

`YES` **See 'Abdominal Pain in Children'**
Younger children may tuck in their legs and make a moaning sound particularly after crying continuously for a long time. Call your doctor.

Is the child taking any medicines or tablets?

`YES` Occasionally some medicines will cause vomiting. Ask your pharmacist. If the child is not able to take any fluids, call your doctor.

Do they have a headache?

`YES` **See 'Meningitis'**
A severe headache such as migraine can cause vomiting. If there is also a blue/black rash call 999.

Is there any pain in their ears?

`YES` **See 'Earache', 'Glue Ear' and 'Middle Ear Infection'**
Infections of the middle ear are common and cause vomiting. If the pain remains after taking paracetamol or decongestants from your pharmacist for one day, call your doctor.

Is the vomit dark brown or does it contain blood? **See 'Abdominal Pain in Children'**
Vomit in young children should never contain blood or brown substances like soil. Give nothing to eat or drink until seen by a doctor. Call 999.

Home treatment

- Give only sips of water or rehydration fluids for the first two hours.

- Increase the amount of clear fluids or rehydration fluids every two hours.

- Build up to a bland diet after eight hours.

- If the condition gets worse or other symptoms develop call your doctor.

Warts and verrucas

Around 5 per cent of school children – one in twenty – will suffer from warts or verrucas. Warts and verrucas are less infectious than we once thought.

Symptoms

Warts can appear anywhere on the body but are most common on the hands and feet. They can also appear at the anus, vagina and penis.

Causes

Dirty skin is not a cause. The papilloma virus actually causes the skin to produce warts. There may be a difference between the viruses which cause hand and feet warts to those which cause genital warts.

Prevention

Wearing protective footwear at public baths may decrease the risk of passing on or picking up the infection.

Complications

Most warts are not dangerous. Verrucas may cause pain when walking. It is worth remembering that genital warts are linked to cervical cancer.

Self-help

Warts and veruccas appear to have a limited lifespan and eventually disappear on their own. It can be a frustrating wait as new warts may appear as the older warts depart. There are a number of wart and verruca removal creams available from your pharmacist. It takes great patience as repeated applications for more than one week are often required.

More help

See your pharmacist or doctor.

Worms

Although we don't like to talk about it, worms are actually very common, particularly in children. It is not a sign of poor hygiene or bad living. Threadworms are the most common. They are itchy, embarrassing but harmless. Roundworms are larger but less common. It is possible to be infected with worms from dogs and cats. Thankfully not so common, these infections can, however, cause blindness. Tapeworms are virtually extinct in the UK.

Symptoms

You may actually see them in your child's motions as tiny white/brown worms in the stool. Itchy bottoms, particularly at night, are the trademark as the female lays its eggs just at the anus around night-time, causing the person to scratch, pick up the eggs, and pass them on or reinfect themselves.

Causes

Infection with worms usually comes from contact with an infected person. They spread very quickly within a family and can remain in families for considerable periods of time without the family realising it.

Prevention

- wash hands after going to the toilet or handling animals
- wash hands before eating

Complications

Threadworms and roundworms do not cause any serious problems. Worms from dogs or cats can, however, cause blindness even in the unborn child if caught by a pregnant woman.

Self-help

You can buy a preparation from your pharmacist across the counter but otherwise you will need a prescription from your doctor.

More help

See your pharmacist or practice nurse. Worm your pets regularly.

Resources and contacts

Association for Post-natal Illness

Provides advice, information and support mainly to
mothers but also runs a support service for partners.
145 Dawes Road, London SW6 7EB
Tel: 020 7386 0868
www.apni.org

The Baby Directory

A commercial site which includes information on aspects of
parenting, including medical advice and new books for children
and their parents.
10 Grove Park Terrace, London W4 3QG
www.babydirectory.com

The Baby Registry

An information site for parents with some specific
sections for dads.
TBR LTD, Haynes, Bedfordshire, MK45 3QE
www.thebabyregistry.co.uk

Babyworld

A comprehensive commercial site from Freeserve which contains
some specific sections for dads.
The Observatory, 36–41 Clerkenwell Close, London EC1R 0AU
www.babyworld.co.uk

British Infertility Counselling Association (BICA)

A professional association offering infertility counselling.
69 Division Street, Sheffield, S1 4GE
Tel: 01342 843880
www.bica.net

CHILD: National Infertility Support Network

Provides support and information for those suffering
from infertility.
Charter House, 3 St Leonards Road, Bexhill on Sea,
East Sussex, TN40 11JA
Tel: 01424 732361
www.child.org.uk

Child Support Agency

The CSA is the government agency that ensures that non-resident
parents contribute towards the financial support of their children.
Great Northern Tower, 17–21 Great Victoria Street, Belfast
BT2 7AD
National Enquiry Helpline: 08457 133 133
www.dss.gov.uk/csa

Dads and Daughters

A US-based organisation which aims to strengthen men's
relationships with their daughters and transform the pervasive
messages that value daughters more for how they look than who
they are.
www.dadsanddaughters.org

divorce.co.uk

Advice on mediation, counselling and the legal aspects of divorce
from a firm of solicitors.
Roger Bamber, Francis House, 112 Hills Road,
Cambridge CB2 1PH
Tel: 01223 222203
www.divorce.co.uk

Donor Conception Network

For advice, information and support on donor insemination.
PO Box 265, Sheffield S3 7YX
Tel: 0208 245 4369
www.dcnetwork.org

Families Need Fathers

Provides legal advice and information mainly about access to
children following divorce or separation.
134 Curtain Road, London EC2A 3AR
Tel: 020 7613 5060
www.fnf.org.uk

Fathers Direct

The national information centre for fatherhood, publishes
FatherWork, a quarterly magazine for fathers and professionals
working with fathers, plus briefing papers. Authors of *The Bounty
Guide to Fatherhood*.
Herald House, Lambs Passage, Bunhill Row, London EC1Y 8TQ
Tel: 020 7920 9491
www.fathersdirect.com

Fathers Network

A US-based organisation that supports fathers and families raising
children with special health care needs and developmental
disabilities.
www.fathersnetwork.org

Fertilisation and Human Embryology Authority

A statutory body which regulates, licenses and collects data on
fertility treatments such as IVF and donor insemination, as well as
human embryo research, in the UK.
HFEA, Paxton House, 30 Artillery Lane, London E1 7LS
Tel: 020 7377 5077
www.hfea.gov.uk

Foundation for the Study of Infant Deaths

For advice and information on preventing cot death and support
following a bereavement.
Artillery House, Artillery Row, London SW1P 1RT
Tel: 020 7222 8001
www.sids.org.uk/fsid

Gingerbread

An organisation which offers practical and emotional support to
lone parent families.
7 Sovereign Court, Sovereign Close, London E1W 3HW.
Tel: 020 7488 9300.
Freephone: 0800 188 4318
www.gingerbread.org.uk/groups

ISSUE: The National Fertility Association

Provides advice, information and support on fertility problems.
114 Lichfield St, Walsall WS1 1SZ
Tel: 01922 722888
www.issue.co.uk

Kidsnet

A guide to days out all over the UK for parents
and their children
www.kidsnet.co.uk

Miscarriage Association

For advice, information and support about miscarriage.
Clayton House, Northgate, Wakefield, West Yorkshire WF1 3JS
Tel: 01924 200799
www.the-ma.org.uk

National Center for Fathering

Provides advice and information for dads (US-based)
www.fathers.com

National Childbirth Trust

For information on antenatal classes, childbirth and local groups
for parents/fathers.
Alexandra House, Oldham Terrace, London W3 6NH
Tel: 0870 444 8707
www.nctms.co.uk

National Council for One Parent Families

Founded in 1918, a national charity working to promote the
interests of lone parents and their children and at the forefront of
change to improve their lives.
255 Kentish Town Road, London NW5 2LX
Tel: 020 7428 5400
www.oneparentfamilies.org.uk

National Fatherhood Initiative

US-based non-profit, non-sectarian, non-partisan organisation that
promotes responsible fatherhood.
www.fatherhood.org

New Dads

A US organisation that provides information for new fathers.
www.newdads.com

New Ways To Work

Provides information and advice on flexible
working arrangements.
26 Shackwell Lane, London E8 2EZ
Tel: 020 7503 3283
www.new-ways.co.uk

NHS Direct

An online health information service (includes child health).
Tel: 0845 4647
www.nhsdirect.nhs.uk

The Parent Company

Runs seminars on parenting; topics include discipline, raising girls and time management for families.
6 Jacob's Well Mews, London W1U 3DY
Tel: 020 7935 9635
www.theparentcompany.co.uk

The Parenting Group

A comprehensive, commercial US site which covers almost everything from pregnancy to pre-school age. The search engine found some 300 references to fathers. Publishes the magazines *Parenting*, *FamilyLife*, and *BabyTalk*.
www.parenting.com

Parentline Plus

Runs a confidential freephone helpline for all parents.
0808 800 2222 (Mon-Fri 9am–9pm, Sat 9.30am–5pm,
Sun 10am–3pm). Textphone/minicom: 0800 783 6783.
Also provides training courses for parents as well as written information.
Unit 520, Highgate Studios, 53–79 Highgate Road,
London NW5 1TL
www.parentlineplus.org.uk

Parents at Work

For information on parents' employment rights.
45 Beech Street, London EC2Y 8AD
Tel: 020 7628 3565
www.parentsatwork.org.uk

Parents Online

Provides information to help parents with children through their primary school years.
21 Universal Marina, Crableck Lane, Sarisbury Green,
Southampton, Hants SO31 7ZN
www.parents.org.uk

Relate

Counselling for relationship and/or sexual problems.
Herbert Gray College, Little Church Street, Rugby,
Warwickshire CV21 3AP
Tel: 01788 57341
www.relate.org.uk

Serene

An advice and information service for parents of excessively
crying, sleepless and demanding babies and young children.
Cry-sis, London WC1N 3XX
Tel: 020 7404 5011
www.our-space.co.uk/serene.htm

Sex Education Forum

Provides information and guidance to parents.
National Children's Bureau, 8 Wakley Street, London EC1V 7QE
Tel: 020 7843 6052
www.ncb.org.uk/sexed.htm

Shared Parenting Information Group (SPIG) UK

An organisation promoting the concept that, following divorce or
separation, mothers and fathers should retain a strong, positive
parenting role with the children spending substantial amounts of
time living with each parent.
www.spig.clara.net

Single and Custodial Father's Network

A US-based online support and networking organisation.
www.scfn.org

Single Parent Action Network UK

Provides information, advice and support to one parent families.
Millpond Baptist Street, Easton, Bristol BS5 0YW
Tel: 0117 9514231
www.spanuk.org.uk

Stay at Home Dads

Provides information and support for househusbands (US-based).
www.slowlane.com

Stonewall

Advice, information and support for gay parents.
46–48 Grosvenor Gardens, London SW1W 0EB
Tel: 020 7881 9440
www.stonewall.org.uk

ukparents.co.uk

An information and community service, mainly aimed at mothers
but with useful information for dads too.
196 Portland Road, Jesmond, Newcastle upon Tyne, NE2 1DJ
Tel: 0870 907 9111
www.ukparents.co.uk

Index